DOWNSTREAM FROM
TROUT FISHING IN AMERICA

Downstream From
Trout Fishing in America

A MEMOIR OF
RICHARD BRAUTIGAN
by
Keith Abbott

CAPRA PRESS
SANTA BARBARA

ACKNOWLEDGMENTS

Parts of this book have appeared in different versions in the following magazines:
California, Clinton Street Quarterly, Exquisite Corpse, Austrian Diner's Club Magazine, and
Review of Contemporary Fiction. A section also was reprinted in the anthology *The Best
of California.* The author also gives special thanks to Seymour Lawrence, Delacorte,
for brief quotes from Brautigan's books: *Rommel Drives Deep Into Egypt, A Confederate
General From Big Sur, Trout Fishing in America,* and *In Watermelon Sugar,* and to
Pocketbooks for quotes from *Sombrero Fallout, The Abortion* and *Revenge of the Lawn.*

PHOTO CREDITS

Front cover courtesy Ianthe Swensen. Photos on back cover, frontispiece, and
author's photo copyright © by Erik Weber. All other photos courtesy Ianthe
Swensen and the Bancroft Library, Berkeley.

Photo editor: Trish Reynales.
Design and typography: Jim Cook/Book Design & Typography

LIBRARY OF CONGRESS CATALOGING-IN-PUBLICATION DATA
Abbott, Keith, 1944–
Downstream from troutfishing in America :
a memoir of Richard Brautigan / by Keith Abbott
ISBN 0-88496-293-8 : $15.95
1. Brautigan, Richard—Biography. 2. Abbott, Keith, 1944- —Friends and associates.
3. Authors, American—20th century—Biography
I. Title. II. Title: Downstream from trout fishing in America.
PS3503.R2736Z57 1989
813′.54—dc19   88-7940 [B] 88-7940

Published by Capra Press
Post Office Box 2068
Santa Barbara, California 93120

Contents

This book is dedicated to all those things that disappear in their becoming.

"It's strange how the simple things in life go on,
while we become difficult."
—Richard Brautigan, *The Abortion*

"Fame falls like a dead hand on an author's shoulder
and it is well for him when it falls only in later life."
—Graham Greene, *The Young Dickens*

Foreword

O ctober 26, 1984, I was moving furniture in a San Francisco loft in preparation for rehearsals of a play of mine that evening when my wife Lani telephoned. She told me Richard Brautigan had been found in his house in Bolinas, apparently dead for many days. Jack Shoemaker, a North Point Press editor, also called to alert me that a local reporter was breaking the news of Brautigan's death to his friends and then harvesting quotes. He warned that she was asking rather nasty and personal questions and several people had been badgered. Brautigan's death was considered sensational. Shoemaker didn't know why, only that Brautigan had died alone.

While I waited for the cast members, I called friends of Richard, but I couldn't contact anyone. When the director arrived, I turned over the rehearsal to him and drove to North Beach, hoping to find someone who knew more about what had happened. My first thought was that Richard had died in an accident, probably due to his drinking.

In North Beach I ran into Tony Dingman. A close friend of Richard over the years, Tony was in shock and had little information to add. As we went around North Beach, those people who had seen Brautigan recently could only repeat that he had been holed up in Bolinas for most of the summer, seeing few visitors. My sense of Richard's recent isolation increased as each of his acquaintances seemed incapable of saying what he had been doing in Bolinas, what his state of mind was, or even how long he had been in town. Almost everyone was drinking, and my sense was that they had been fried even before the news of Brautigan's death. Sad as his fate was, this aura of alcoholic oblivion surrounding his recent past depressed me.

When I got home, the late news on television spoke of a gunshot wound. I had a bad time with that. Only after Lani talked to me for a few hours was I able to face that Richard had committed suicide.

In the following days the local newspapers ran a string of sensational items on Brautigan, calling him "the literary celebrity of the hippie era." Almost all of the people quoted were not in San Francisco, but in Montana, Los Angeles or New York. A strange, shadowy sense crept over me that the local memory of Brautigan had been wiped clean. His reputation as a loner was repeated. A feeling was reinforced that if this man ever had friends, they had deserted him and let him die alone. In the public press, his past as a California literary figure seemed to have been swept downstream and smashed, in the same deadly manner as his recent months had been fragged in the minds of his North Beach drinking buddies.

On the 31st of October a wake for Brautigan was held at Enrico's cafe in North Beach. For me, the gathering pulled together a sense of his life. The range of people was wide and various, from movie directors, such as Francis Ford Coppola and Phil Kaufman, to other writers and artists, among them Jeremy Larner, Curt Gentry, Bruce Conner and Don Carpenter, and to his friends including some of his old Haight-Ashbury cronies, such as ecologist Peter Berg. I kept having a thought, one that others voiced, too, "Wouldn't it be great if Richard were here. He'd really love this."

With this collective idea came the undercurrent of guilt we all shared. Brautigan's good friend, the painter Marcia Clay, articulated it so well. "What everybody keeps saying is why didn't we do something? But what people forget is that they did make attempts. Plenty tried to help him, and none of us could."

Early in 1985, when the national magazines *Rolling Stone* and *Vanity Fair* published their accounts of Brautigan's life, the sensational aspects were trumpeted. In the *Rolling Stone* piece, bold headlines spoke of a youthful stay in a mental hospital and alleged S&M bondage. The ghastly story of his body decomposing for weeks in his Bolinas house was punched up along with his last ugly days playing the alcoholic geek in California bars. What made Brautigan's writing unique and, for a time, so amazingly popular, was glossed over. His early persona of the trendy California author also took the focus, but this time around the flowerchild image was cut with a heavy dose of '80s cynicism, as if personal eccentricity were always perversely nasty and created from the pressure of something inevitably sordid.

Those accounts shortchanged the Richard Brautigan I knew, a man who cared for his friends, who was generous to a fault at times, and a man who liked to be kind to people. I missed the dedicated author of his best novels, too, the man who worked his prose over and over to get the simplicity and clarity he loved.

Shortly after these lurid reports, a much more positive picture emerged when a celebration of his writing was broadcast on National Public Radio. This was devoted almost entirely to interviews with his readers, not Brautigan's critics or ex-friends. A fan told how, as a student, he and his friends used phrases from *Trout Fishing In America* such as "Kool-aid Wino," for passwords into private worlds not acknowledged in their public life. Richard's best writing radiated that joyous sense of being in on a secret, and this was strongly present in his life, too. It is with this notion—of recovering a secret past—that I wrote this memoir of Brautigan during the eighteen years we knew each other.

Keith Abbott

I. San Francisco
1966-1967

I n 1965 I came from Seattle to live in Monterey. There I made friends with Price Dunn, the model for Lee Mellon, free-spirited hero of Richard's first published novel, *A Confederate General From Big Sur*. Price never talked about his role in the novel, but spoke of Richard from time to time, usually in general terms, vaguely hinting about his eccentric life. Price's comments provoked my interest. The last time Richard dropped in on Price in Monterey, I'd been in town, but missed his visit. Their freefall through the New Monterey bars still had the locals talking. As much as Brautigan's poetry and novel had interested me, what really intrigued me was that if Price regarded someone as an eccentric, then he must be odd, because Price was the most charming, erratic, poetic and haphazard person I'd ever met.

Early in March of 1966, when my girlfriend Lani's unemployment ran out, we moved up the coast to San Francisco and jobhunted. Only chance and cheap rent landed us on 777 Haight Street, because neither of us had any idea what was going on in the neighborhood. A few weeks after we settled in, Price drove up from Monterey and took me over to Geary Street for my first meeting with Richard.

When Richard opened the door to his apartment, my impression was that he looked like a cross between Mark Twain and a heron. More than anything that he said, his physical presence in the shadowy surroundings impressed me.

15

It was as if a Twain stand-in from a Gold Rush flick had wandered onto a low-budget Gothic horror set.

Hung above the long dark hallway to his back apartment were faded pink curtains, hiding the peeling paint on the ceiling. Posters of readings were tacked up on the water-stained walls along with odd bits of handwritten paper, such as a fading sheet with the scrawled message, "Today is the first day of your life." Through the open door to Richard's writing room I could see an old IBM typewriter on a table, a grey tattered curtain covering a small window, and piles of magazines, manuscripts and books stacked all over the floor.

Brautigan led us down to the kitchen and once we were there, Price joked with him, dusting off their old routines and telling of his newest adventures. Whenever someone told a good story, Richard tried to minimize his tall and long-legged presence. He'd cross his hands in front of him, with arms held in, to better act the unobtrusive listener. (His pose on the cover of his novel, "The Abortion," gives an approximation of this stance.) When he was in his listening mode, Brautigan had a funny, bird-like way of standing to one side, peering down from his six foot-four-inch height. On this imaginary shoreline, he would break into a conversation, neatly spearing some comment and spinning off into an outrageous and fantastic digression.

While Price and Richard traded jokes in the kitchen, I nosed around the apartment. The front room contained a bed. At its foot stood a short stepladder with tassled red velvet on the top platform. A rusty woodstove camped in front of the unused fireplace. Cabinet shelves were loaded with books, a collection of rusty keys, pennies, rocks, feathers, Mason jars and a cracked, silver hand mirror. A sentimental picture of a stallion's head framed by a lucky horseshoe had printed under it the slogan "Fuck Death." Hell's Angels mementos, posters and shoulder patches were scattered around. Strange macho signals, I thought at the time, for a man whose poetry seemed so fey, romantic and fantastic.

An Army issue, khaki-colored trout fishing manual was propped against the wall by a wicker chair. Richard noticed me looking at it and darted in from the kitchen. This manual turned out to be something he took great delight in showing off, reveling in the disparity between the dead official language and its lively quicksilver subject.

Now, at that time, *Trout Fishing in America* was unpublished, so I didn't know why Richard would take the pains to read parts of the Army fishing manual to me. At first it was merely another one of his eccentricities.

The kitchen held the most rudimentary cookware. The cupboard was a bachelor display of easy, one-can meals, such as Chef Boy-Ar-Dee Spaghetti, and the refrigerator was a mausoleum for condiments. Over the table hung the kitchen's only decoration, a funky, butcher paper and crayon poster for Richard's first reading of *Trout Fishing*. When I saw that, I made the connection between the trout memorabilia and his writing.

Without Price acting as catalyst, it would have been difficult to make friends with Richard, he was reserved with strangers. Because of his shyness, he seldom talked about his friends directly and usually referred to them in terms of objects, using things as symbols for what he admired. These things developed into comedy routines, and Price had brought from Monterey the object of one of their running jokes, Willard. Originally made by Stanley Fullerton, a mutual friend in Santa Cruz, Willard was a goofy-looking papier mâché bird. About four feet high and painted red, white, orange and black, Willard had big saucer eyes, a huge beak and a round pot-bellied body. Usually Willard was propped up in a corner, his long spindly legs crossed and his body tilted out in an Ichabod Crane stance, one which curiously mimicked Brautigan's way of standing.

"Willard's been getting lonesome for you," Price told Richard in his best southern idiot voice. "It's time for you to take care of Willard again, Richard."

The game was to leave Willard at the other person's house. Willard would get hidden in Richard's closet or shoved at the last minute under a tarp on Price's pickup, and over the years their Willard Ditching became quite an elaborate practical joke between them.

Another one of their routines involved Price's coffee. Since

I'd already experienced this concoction, I appreciated Richard's efforts at describing the effect of drinking it. Being poor, Richard used instant coffee. Price always made "sheepherder's coffee" using the strongest brands, such as commercial Italian espresso or Yuban. Price would throw the grounds into boiling water and let them steep. After sprinkling cold water on top, he'd blow off the scum and pour. This coffee was always electrifying because Price, an extravagant person, never used too little. Richard would take a sip and consider its effect on his nervous system. "Most coffee makes you want to get up and do things. Price's coffee pins you to a chair and lets you listen to your nerve ends fry," he'd say. "You know, Price, maybe this morning I'll use an ax on that novel, instead of a typewriter."

With the coffee working on me, I left Price and Richard to their comic routines and went to the bathroom. Brautigan's bathtub had a tear-shaped rust mark under the nozzle. On the toilet was a copy of Baker's Ernest Hemingway bio. On one wall was a glossy Beatles poster and on the other, above the toilet paper, was a royalty statement from Grove Press stating that *A Confederate General From Big Sur* had sold 743 copies. What Richard thought about this was easy to guess from its position.

Since it was a sunny day in San Francisco, Price drove us over to Golden Gate Park in his 1956 Chevy truck. While we walked around the de Young Museum, the three of us already created a stream of running jokes and allusions, inventing myths for each other.

That day Price became a subject of comic routines between Richard and I, functioning in the same way that coffee did for the two of them. Among Price's admirable traits was that he had no trouble with sensual pleasure. He was an Alabama hedonist who loved good meals, good books and who appreciated interesting women and classical music. While Price could play the role of a macho hero, telling stories of barroom brawls and startling seductions, he was also a romantic dreamer like Richard. What separated Price from Richard was that Price often acted as if reality and fantasy were exactly the same.

Of the three of us, Price had the most fantastic imagination.

Even better, because he was not an author, he acted upon his fantasies. Like many writers, Richard seldom acted on his impulses and he envied Price's ability to do this. Brautigan's willful, delicate side fueled his writing, but he admired what he wasn't—a strong masculine presence.

After wandering around the park, we ended up at the Steinhardt Aquarium. There, in front of the garfish tank, Richard and I shared our first Price Dunn adventure.

"Garfish!" Price shouted. He pushed his way through the tourists and stood beaming at the fish, as if they were old buddies. "You know we used to catch them down South?" Price shouted back at us.

Richard and I drifted in behind him. A few of the tourists shifted into postions of flight: they didn't like the looks of us.

This was in the days before Golden Gate Park became littered with hippies, so our appearance was an anomaly. Richard was wearing his battered grey hat and his vest with various emblems pinned to it, almost exactly as he would appear on the cover of *Trout Fishing In America*. I was in a large white knee-length smock with the word HIPPO embroidered on the back. Price was in his usual jeans and T-shirt, wearing broken and taped granny glasses, and at six-feet-three inches, he looked like a Hell's Angel on a lunch break.

Price continued to wave at the huge fish swimming around the tank behind their improbable alligator snouts. "Gars!" Price hooted. "Why we used to land them just as big as that. And you know how we caught them?"

Neither Richard nor I said anything. We were watching the tourists nervously watching Price.

"First you get a corn cob," Price explained, oblivious to the people backing away from him. "And then you get a long bamboo pole, you know the kind. Put a line on it with a hook and then you put the corn cob on the hook and throw it in the river."

Price beamed at the fish, cast an imaginary corn cob into the fish tank, and then his voice dropped down into a whisper. "And when that old gar comes up for the corn cob, you can see that old gar real clear." He straightened up out of his fishing stance for a second, sending the crowd back another step, as his voice rose in an aside, "Hell, they're as big as a house anyway."

Then his voice dropped to a whisper again and he crouched, showing how the pole was held. "So, when the gar comes up for your corn cob . . . and you can see them real clear, why you," Price shouted, "you drop the pole, pick up your rifle and you shoot them!"

The minute that Price said he shot the fish, the tourists fled, sure that he and his two weird henchmen were about to relive those childhood memories, whipping out guns from under their clothes and blasting away at the fish tanks.

Richard and I looked at each other. Both of us were Northwest fishermen, raised with a code for catching fish. We took Price by the arm and led him away from the gars. Later, we talked about how we both had the same thought: that this was the most bizzare way to fish that we had ever heard: you don't shoot fish, you hook them.

From then on, Richard and I were fast friends, bonded together by our mutual fascination with Price's outrageous and often improbable life. When Price told us something marvelous—like how one of his boyhood chores in Alabama was unchaining his mad uncle from the attic and fastening him to a tree during storms because the rain calmed him down so wonderfully—Richard and I would joke about who got rights for any future writing.

"You got that one?"

"No, you better take that one. It's too much for me to handle."

Despite his shyness, Richard did have a great capacity to let people into his life. His fiercest allegiance was to the imagination. Once he felt you shared that with him, then his loyalty was final. That, and our mutual fascination with Price, first formed our friendship.

Whenever we got together, Richard asked for the latest news of Price's scandals or scores. Had he sold that broken-down motorcycle for the fourth time? (Price had already sold it three times to three different people and somehow always managed to keep the wreck.) Had he torn out any more interior walls in his house? What ever happened to that cache of Weston photographs he'd found in a Big Sur outhouse? Was Price still driving around with the rare orchids from that Pebble Beach gardening job dying in the bed of his pickup? What about his Nash Metropolitan? Did it still require that big drink of brake fluid every morning? And how was Price's phone now listed: under Commander Ralph G. Gore, William Bonney, Delmer Dibble or Jesse James?

My first stay in San Francisco lasted from spring through fall of 1966. I worked for Pan Am at the airport and Lani found a job at Red Cross. She had lived in the city for two years before we paired up in Monterey and so she knew its pleasures and delights. This was my first experience with city living. For me the new food and new people and close-knit neighborhoods blended into the flowering of the Haight-Ashbury and the psychedelic revolution.

This time wasn't completely idyllic. The Fillmore district rioted and the National Guard patrolled the streets a few weeks before we left town. Still, I came to regard those months on the lower Haight as the best that urban civilization can offer: vistas, an active street life, neighborhood parks and good ethnic food.

From our first walks past Yerba Buena Park, through the Haight and into Golden Gate Park, the signs of an ongoing liberation were clear. LSD was still legal. In Seattle I had taken a lot of acid and dealt it too, but when I came to California I had sworn off it, perversely enough. I felt I had learned as much as I could from psychedelics. One stroll through the Panhandle clued me in that I was member of something larger than being another struggling writer in San Francisco. From the first few weeks I had the sense that we had tumbled into an historical event. Whatever this history would eventually mean, I thought, it really *felt* wonderful.

Robin Williams jokes that if you can remember this time, then you weren't there. It isn't really true for me. 1966 recalls the wet touch of early morning fog and the perfume of eucalyptus, and I see again the smiling people in bright clothes who drifted around the Panhandle, nodding at the world so re-assuringly. Such an aura of confidence, grace and mystery lasted only into 1967, but the communal sense of breaking through to a better world was there, and it was exhilarating. My delight in the high rooms of the San Francisco apartments was born then, too, along with my love of ornate mouldings and tall windows. From the attic cupolas rose fantasies of the perfect writing room.

These cheerful sunny flats inspired me. For decoration in our drab digs on Haight Street I stole from my Pan Am job rolls of destination tape, each country or city a different color. With these I formed a whirling wall mosiac in our kitchen and tried to bring some sense of light into our dark flat, but really only succeeded in horrifying my landlord. My youthful love affair with San Francisco coincided with my fascination with Richard's life, and for me the two became inextricably entwined.

On my days off, we'd meet at my apartment before starting our travels up Haight Street to the park. While we bummed around, he told me a few things about his recent past. During the previous two years, Richard had been living on advances from his Grove Press contract. Via a four novel option, they had bought his first novel, *Trout Fishing In America,* and his second, *A Confederate General From Big Sur,* but only published the latter. His third novel, *In Watermelon Sugar,* had been rejected, and there remained his fourth, *The Abortion,* which he had finished shortly before I met him. When that novel was rejected, he was no longer on contract, and Richard scuffled every day for his rent and food.

Even though busfare was only 15 cents, Richard would walk from Geary Street over to my Haight Street place below Divisadero, a distance of twenty blocks. Once I asked him if he would like a sandwich before we hiked up the hill to Golden Gate Park. The way he said yes and ate it stayed in my mind. From then on, I would have some food ready when he dropped by, and we would eat before we went on our rambles.

While he never complained about his money situation, he also remained mysterious about it. During the time I spent strolling around the Haight with him, he never discussed his cash problems. Price told me that Richard worked one or two days a month for some strange inventor, washing test tubes and mixing chemicals in a lab. Before rent day, Richard would check down at City Lights to see if any of his books of poetry on consignment—*Lay The Marble Tea* or *The Octopus Frontier*— had sold. Then he would make the rounds of North Beach bars and put the touch on anyone for food money. Later, when he was wealthy and a fixture at Enrico's outdoor cafe on Broadway, I never saw Richard refuse a panhandler.

After we became good friends, one of Richard's routines with Price soon became one of ours. If either of us lacked money, all that had to be said was, "Do you have that dollar you owe me?" and the money was exchanged.

Strangely enough, given this poverty, wedded to my memory of Brautigan are my first experiences with marvelous food and expensive drink. Whenever we had money, we spent it on the best—especially if the ever-generous Price had made a windfall, something that often happened with his luck of the Irish.

In the spring of 1966 Price's girlfriend, Baby Katherine, got an insurance check from an auto accident. To celebrate, Price bought a bargain 1950 Studebaker for $25 from some broke voyager recently returned from Mexico. He and Katherine drove to San Francisco "to put on the feed bag." Lani and I were picked up at our Haight Street apartment before Price motored over to North Beach to meet Richard for some Chinese food. Of course, Price hadn't bothered to clean out the former owner's junk from the Mexican vacation so I cleared the back seat, pushing spare car parts, old sleeping bags, and empty tequila bottles on the foor.

As Price barrelled onto the freeway at the Fell Street entrance, he was so excited about our feast that night, he began shouting out the dishes that we were about to taste. Unfortunately, each time Price changed the menu, he changed lanes. "No," he'd yell, "Mu Shu pork!" Swerve, "And *then* the Tea-smoked Duck!"

Somewhere on the Embarcadero freeway, Lani's expression

of concern for our safety changed to utter horror when a huge, hairy spider crawled out by her feet, a little hitchhiker from South of the Border. Without interrupting Price's oratorio or further disturbing his driving, I flattened it with a hub cap.

That night, Richard and Price introduced me to Chinese rarities, oyster sauce chicken wings, sharkfin soup, and Mongolian beef. After dinner we did a crawl of North Beach bars and cafes, sampling Pouilly Fuissé, Ficklin's Port, Grand Marnier and Armagnac, and in this cheerful company I tasted my first zabaglione and chocolate mousse.

The one amazing constant about Richard in 1966 was his optimism. Given his hand-to-mouth existence, the word doesn't really give the heroic aura that his daily life seemed to radiate for me. As near as I could discover, Richard's daily schedule was to write in the morning, make a few phone calls, and then launch himself into the serendipity of San Francisco life. Moseying from casual acquaintance to friend, from bar to cafe, he clearly regarded his daily life as its own work of art. Some of this art was captured in writing, some wasn't. He didn't agonize over this loss. Sometimes he celebrated it. Brautigan's writing and his life style certainly seemed at odds with his prevailing feeling of incipient good luck. As much as I admired *A Confederate General* I couldn't imagine his writing finding a large enough audience to sustain his life. I wasn't alone in this. Very few people could imagine then that such an audience would spring up overnight.

The sense that anything was possible permeated San Francisco during those joyful early days in the Haight-Ashbury. My friends and I felt we were creating another minority in a town full of minorities. The best-case scenario was that when the neighborhood was ours, the city would acknowledge us, as Italians or Japanese or Hispanics had been eventually recognized and tolerated. The fantasy was that the City would let the heads be.

When the first glimmerings of the psychedelic revolution were seen daily, from the Fillmore posters to the clothes people were wearing, there seemed to be a wonderful collective sigh of relief. Implicit in that sigh was the notion: Now we're going to have our own world, (or as the poet Philip Whalen wrote, make "an electrical magical Tibet"). The feeling that something great, earthshaking and wonderful was about to happen seemed to invade every activity. This notion was infectious, no matter how broken-down and hopeless one's circumstances, and it wasn't only an illusion of the stoned. The daily doping during the later days of the Haight wasn't happening among my friends—simply because the supply wasn't that steady and the inclination wasn't there.

How Richard, or all those other strange folks populating the Panhandle, managed to survive or even make the rent, fascinated me. As a young writer myself, I was impressed that Brautigan seemed to exist mostly on money he made from his writing. In all my twenty-two years I had never met a writer who supported himself by his work. All the writers I had met were teachers or had jobs doing something unrelated to writing. Brautigan, determined to make it as a writer on his own terms, was my idea of a dedicated artist.

At the time Richard hardly ever talked about his childhood. From Price's stories about him, I learned we had some things in common. We had been born in Tacoma, Washington. We both were Aquarians, his birthdate January 30 and mine February 2, and we both lived through working-class Northwest childhoods. Richard and I used to joke about how improbable it was that we were artists, when there were no examples in our backgrounds: only stump ranchers, farmers, loggers, fry cooks and commercial fishermen.

Richard took great pride in the fact that he did create against these odds. Often he claimed the power of his friends' art as being in proportion to the struggle for its birth. He claimed strength from the rejections he suffered along the way, and was determined that they would only fuel him for more work.

"None of my friends were ever given much early encouragement," he was fond of saying. "No one ever thought they'd do anything good."

In 1966, these were brave ideas from a man whose only published novel had been remaindered. He had three unpublished novels, no agent and no publisher, and yet, most of the time he seemed supremely confident of his talent and work. His optimistic attitude appeared naive to his San Francisco writer friends. There was a tendency to discount the possibility of his work ever becoming important. To them, Brautigan's experience of the world, his dirt-poor background and his social isolation, seemed too limited. But one only needs a small patch of turf to make a world.

While discussing the early days of his friendship with Hart Crane, Malcom Cowley makes a pertinent point about this class distinction. He writes that at first he thought Crane not very bright because "he hadn't the quick competence I had come to expect of my friends, most of whom had been scholarship boys in college.... I hadn't yet learned to appreciate [Crane's] single-minded devotion to writing poems or his capacity for working at each of them week after week until it had assumed the exact new shape of which he dreamed."

A lot of people, myself included, reacted in a similiar way to Brautigan's character. Even though I was almost ten years younger, I felt protective toward him since Richard seemed so awkward, so uneducated and unworldly. But, I also imagined myself to be in a similar position, even though I wasn't. I had a family and some college education. Since I was a young writer with no particular experience to write about, Richard's desire to be an author seemed heroic. His subject matter was whatever his own fantastic imagination could invent from limited experiences of his life. He hadn't led a life of adventure or social success, he had lived on the fringe.

This fringe status defined many of Brautigan's relationships. Price Dunn often acted as a big brother, gently correcting Richard's sometimes fantastic misconceptions of the world. During social events Brautigan could act the part of a county bumpkin. Yet on other occasions, he displayed a quick apprehension of the prevalent social dynamics. For example, one evening in the early 1970s, I was accompanying him on some minor errands and we ran into a large party of artists, among them the writers Robert Creeley, Bobbie Louise

Hawkins and Joanne Kyger. The party was fresh out of a gallery opening and looking for something to do. Brautigan spontaneously invited them to dinner, at his expense, remarking that he wanted to return the many favors some of these people had performed for him. Since he had recently become a financially solvent writer, the gesture was an invitation to share in those rewards, and it was appreciated as such. At the restaurant, he was a genial host, directing the conversation from one writer to another, and enjoying their talk. But the evening ended disastrously when we returned to his Geary Street apartment for a nightcap, and someone asked him about his recent work. It was as if a switch had been pulled. Richard brought out a long fragmented sequence of poems and he proceeded to ruin what had been a happy event with a reading of his most alienated and depressed poetry. Richard was always capable of living at the edge of his nerve ends and making that pay off, but as with most artists, his social skills often would depend on the degree of his self-absorption at any moment.

Because Brautigan's fiction seemed to be simple fantasy, I assumed at first that his personality reflected this, too. But I was soon disabused of that notion. Richard was probably the most psychologically complicated and most willful person I've ever met. Even in his whimsical moments, he pursued his fantasies with determination.

That will was what made Brautigan different from a mere oddball: his fierce devotion to his craft. William Blake reminds us, "If a fool were to persist in his folly, he would become wise." As one of my students once commented: "How can a fool persist?"

More important than Brautigan's persistence was his situation. What was hard for me to understand in those budding slaphappy days of the Haight-Ashbury was that Richard had to succeed as an artist. With no family beyond a divorced wife and their daughter, he had developed few economic skills and embraced no society beyond that of his fellow writers and North Beach hangers-on. If he didn't succeed as a writer, there was literally nothing else for him to do with his life. From his point of view, it was all or nothing.

During our Haight Street apartment days, my social circumstances changed. Lani and I had got married and she was pregnant with our daughter. Although I didn't discuss it, the pressures of fatherhood were on my mind. Coming from working class Irish and Polish parents, I thought of my role as being a provider. With my background that meant getting harnessed to a job, sidetracking any dreams I might have, and "knuckling down under," as my father used to say. However, in the Haight-Ashbury, I was enjoying the cosmopolitan and artistic world of San Francisco and witnessing the birth of what seemed to be a whole other way to live. Although my cultural roots impelled me toward socially responsible fatherhood, my plans were to quit my job, move to sunny Monterey, live on unemployment, write books, and in general violate the creed that my parents had worked so hard to instill in me. All of which I proceeded to do that September.

During Christmas of 1966, we left Monterey and returned to Tacoma for the holidays. On the drive up, my sister turned over her Volkswagon van on the highway. The van's repairs took a long time, and we were stuck in the Northwest without enough money. To finance our unexpected stay, I dealt LSD to college friends in Bellingham. For old time's sake I also took a small dose around six one morning. I arrived back home in Tacoma that night and, in the sunny optimism of my tripping, I decided to level with my family about my resolutions.

When I told my father I planned to be a writer, he informed me, "Then you'll be nothing but a parasite for the rest of your life."

This was not what I hoped to hear.

My parents' perspective makes me recognize that the portrait I've drawn of Brautigan is the familiar one of a starving artist living in a run-down apartment, with only optimism for support. This could have functioned as a confirmation of my father's dire predictions for my fate, but it didn't at the time.

What made Richard an exception was the same thing that made his books fun to read: his imagination.

A day in San Francisco with him became a vacation from those struggles, a chance to step back, examine my assumptions and see if there was some way to invent a life that would allow me to become a writer. Richard was not a practical model, but I wasn't really looking for practicality. I was looking for inspiration.

In those days going around with Brautigan was like traveling inside one of his novels. With friends Richard talked just as he wrote. Outrageous metaphors and looney tune takes were commonplace; one-liners, bizarre fantasies, and lightning asides darted out of him one after another. He loved to improvise verbal games but he would do them deadpan, pretending to have no humor at all. He seldom cracked up. Sometimes we would spend hours trading skewed dialogue from a Bogart movie or talking to each other in weird rewrites of Beatle lyrics.

Richard's willfullness played a part in these routines, too. Although he was open to inspired changes, he liked to control the guidelines for these games. He often dictated what the shared reality was to be for the day. For example, one afternoon as we passed the hamburger stand outside his apartment, he sniffed. "Ah—the smell of grease on the winter wind." Then, very solemnly, "Li Po, I believe."

While we went about our errands for the rest of the day, we improvised fake Chinese poems, always careful to end them with ficticious attributions and the pompous phrase, "I believe." One of Richard's favorite expressions for these routines was that they "disappeared in their becoming."

He believed in the magic and spirit of play and worked very hard to get that quality in his writing.

In his life this playfulness often came easily, his wit sharp and yet grounded on the reality of any scene. A good example is the day I left Haight Street to return to Monterey.

The night before, one of my old Northwest friends arrived in town. Released from an unhappy marriage and toting a bag of housewife diet pills, she was ready to sample the Haight-

Ashbury night life. We ricochetted between two parties, one on Haight street for my poet and printer friend, Clifford Burke, and another around the corner for the poet John Logan, with whom I'd studied at the University of Washington. While I showed her the town, I drank a lot of beer and smoked two packs of Lucky Strikes. The next day I had an alcohol, amphetamine and nicotine hangover. Feeling like death warmed over, I was standing in the middle of my apartment, looking at the boxes of stuff, when the doorbell rang. It was Richard.

"Need some help moving?" Then he took a closer look at me.

"You do need some help," he said, and he took off his Levi jacket, propped open the front door, and began to carry the boxes down to my truck while I turned in circles in the front room.

That was the day I stopped smoking. My tongue was raw from all the Luckies. Each time I reached for a pack, my tongue ached so bad I couldn't force myself to light up. (As it turned out, I never smoked cigarettes again.)

Brautigan always had a deft hand with hangover patients. While Richard carried my gear down to the truck, he talked to me, turning my predicament into a little short story.

"You look like walking death," he said. "When I'm done with this, we'll take you out back and shoot you. Maybe we could just burn you at the stake. We could take you to Golden Gate Park and give the tourists up there a human torch to look at."

This fantasy amused Richard and he watched me carefully as I reacted in my slow dull way to what he had said before embroidering the story further.

"They'll be having a picnic on the grass and the kids will gather around you and say things like, 'Hey daddy, come over here and look at the human torch!' "

"With all that leftover alcohol inside you," he said, giving me the professional once-over, "I'd say that you'll burn for at least a day."

Following in Price's footsteps, I bought an old Chevy truck before we left the city. In Monterey I started my own gardening and hauling business to supplement our unemployment checks. Lani and I were happy in our shack on Spencer Street overlooking the ruined canneries and the bay. Living was cheap, and we had enough spare cash for drives up the coast to San Francisco. On our visits Richard and I continued our travels around the city. We dropped off things at the Diggers' store, the Free Frame of Reference, and participated in the amazing loose goosey days of the Haight. Richard continued to include me in the literary life, introducing me to local writers, such as playwright Michael McClure, novelist Don Carpenter and poet Lew Welch.

Because of his own neglected status during these days, Richard had developed a wry sense of humor about publishing. I loved to draw comments from him. Once, when we were out to xerox a poetry manuscript of mine, I deadpanned that I was thinking of hopping on a redeye flight and taking it to the New York publisher myself. I asked him what he thought of my book's chances.

"Oh, I'd give your book about the same odds," Richard said, "as I'd give a crippled virgin at a Shriner's convention."

When we talked literature, Brautigan set self-limits, usually confining himself to works that had directly helped him write. Since I'd attended some creative writing classes at the University of Washington, I was much more used to the kind of theoretical talk that fueled seminars than Richard's careful comments.

The poet Jack Spicer was Brautigan's most serious contemporary influence. Spicer had edited an early draft of *Trout Fishing In America.* The actor Gail Chugg remembers Spicer going around North Beach and telling people, "Richard's written a marvelous little book." Eventually Spicer arranged for *Trout Fishing's* first public readings, two consecutive nights at a local church. Richard loved the poems in Spicer's book *Language,* and could recite some from memory.

Brautigan revered Sherwood Anderson's story, "Death in the Woods," for its simple and clear language. To him I owe my discovery of Isaac Babel. Richard seldom loaned out his books, but when I told him I hadn't read Babel, he handed me the

Collected Stories and told me to go and immediately read "Guy De Maupasssant." He also had Hemingway's collection of journalism, *By-Line*. In it there are some rare examples of Hemingway's playfulness with language, and I find an echo of them in Brautigan's early prose.

The Greek Anthology he recommended for models of brevity and emotional concision and he owned a complete set. Generally his library was a writer's library, only literary works, very little criticism. The rare anthologies or textbooks were either gifts or comp copies.

A modern poet Brautigan promoted was Kenneth Fearing. Richard thought his work minor, but interesting enough to merit not being forgotten. At the time Richard had to fear that this was the way he would go himself, if he didn't have some luck. This surfaces in the opening chapters of *The Abortion*, written in 1966. The protagonist mans the front desk for a library of unpublished manuscripts. The authors bring in and register their failures, then the manuscripts are put on shelves to be eventually trucked to some caves for storage. The directory of deposited books has always seemed a brilliant catalogue of social comment on the forlorn life of unpublished writers, but after this fantasy beginning, the narrative eventually thinned out and never really sustained its premise. Partly this letdown occurred because Richard finished the book in a last-ditch attempt to fulfill the four book option of his Grove Press contract. And partly it was a signal that his initial inspiration for fiction had dried up after he produced four novels.

In the fall of 1966 Brautigan mentioned that his remaindered novel, *A Confederate General From Big Sur*, was selling well at Moe's Books in Berkeley. This was really the only positive note for his career at that time. In *The Abortion* Richard characteristically inflated this private hope into a myth. At the end of the novel the character says that he is becoming a cult figure in Berkeley. That this flicker of public recognition from the sale of his remaindered books might signal a turnaround in his career now carries a weird echo since it presaged his own rise from Haight-Ashbury cult fame to national prominence.

II. Digger Days

B rautigan's career began its rise because of the Haight-Ashbury group, The Diggers. Branching off from the San Francisco Mime Troupe, this loose collection of civic anarchists tried to effect social change through street theater and leaderless events. At first Richard's whole-hearted involvement in the Diggers' social programs was puzzling to me. The Diggers' anarchism attracted him the most, but he admired their public idealism, too. This was an uneasy alliance. Like most Digger collaborations, it created mixed blessings and ambiguous results.

One day Richard called me and asked for the use of my truck. When I arrived at his apartment, he was busy making phone calls and setting up appointments. With a great show of enthusiasm he told me that our task was to pick up a load of pants for the Diggers' store, The Free Frame of Reference. Then he told me the story of how "a socialite woman" came to the Diggers' store and tried to donate a check. Now, at the Free Frame of Reference, it was a point of honor that no one would cop to being in charge, or even to being a Digger. But Emmett Grogan, one of the Diggers, was pointed out to this woman.

With great glee, Richard acted out the woman offering the check, and then Grogan taking and tearing it up. This gesture impressed the woman and she asked what, besides money, could be given. Grogan told her that clothes were needed. She figured out that, because no one was boss, neither would anyone sign for any deliveries at the Free Frame of Reference.

35

So the woman arranged for a load of factory seconds to be dropped off at her house.

Grogan and the Diggers were heroes to Brautigan and this tale delighted him. With a little probing, I found out this version was a second-hand one. For all his acting, Brautigan had not actually witnessed the event. How and why he got the detail of ferrying the clothes back to the Diggers was unclear. All this was typical of Richard's involvement with the Diggers, which was fueled by equal parts of fantasy, idealism and self-promotion.

The outcome of this generosity was quite typically ambiguous, too. We picked up the cartons of pants at an expensive Jackson Street address and trucked them to the Digger garage. After everyone congratulated themselves on this demonstration of Digger mystique and knowhow, Richard and some others took off for an important meeting. I hung around to see what happened to the pants. At first a few people found their sizes and got some new clothes for themselves. Then the word got out on the street, the hustlers descended and armloads of pants were hauled off, probably for resale in Golden Gate Park. Soon the boxes were empty and nothing was left in the free store except the usual ugly castoffs. So many of the Digger events that I witnessed were like this: a few whitecaps of communal concern in a tidal wave of stoned runaways and street hustlers.

Brautigan wasn't blind to the ambiguity of the efforts, but while the Diggers' Communication Company continued publication of his work, he discounted or ignored the less mythic aspects of the Diggers' programs. This mutual admiration was a welcome change from the reception Brautigan's work had previously been given by the North Beach establishment of Beat writers.

In his *Rolling Stone* article after Brautigan's death, Lawrence Wright makes much of the fact that Brautigan was a fringe figure in North Beach. Allen Ginsberg had hung the nickname of Bunthorne on him. A Gilbert and Sullivan character, Bunthorne is a synonym for a precious and winsome poet who indulges in "idle chatter of a transcendental kind." This was apt, given that Brautigan's early poems were perfect Bunthorne productions, concocted of brief whimsical thoughts of a metaphorical and ephemeral nature. His public Bunthorne persona as a poet often exposed Brautigan to ridicule—of which Ginsberg's was perhaps the kindest among his North Beach mentors. Since he continued to publish mainly his poems, people could not reconcile those sometimes simple-minded lyrics with what seemed to be Brautigan's inflated self-regard.

Because his private industry as a fiction writer wasn't evident to his North Beach acquaintances, it was easy to dismiss him. But after Brautigan labored through what he later estimated were seventeen total revisions of *Trout Fishing In America,* he became well aware of his own peculiar gifts and he took himself seriously as a writer. When Brautigan hit the jackpot as a novelist, his North Beach status as a fringe poet, the social inconsequence of the Haight and the maintenance of his naive poet role via his book covers contrived to present a media image that he never did shake.

Like Brautigan's literary reputation in 1966, the Diggers Communication Company was a fly-by-night operation, consisting of Gestetner mimeo machines and a Gestafax stencil cutter. Besides newsletters, manifestos, and comic books, the Communication Company published a few literary works by writers other than Brautigan. One novel, *Informed Sources* by Willard Bain, eventually was reprinted by a New York publisher. The titles of Brautigan's poetry broadsides are indications of their contents: "Karma Repair Kit," "The Beautiful Poem," "Love Poem," "Flowers For Those You Love." His free book of poetry was titled with a trendy utopian cybernetic slant, *All Watched Over By Machines of Loving Grace.* While such productions did nothing to drive up Brautigan's literary stock, the Diggers mimeo press solved three of Brautigan's practical problems as an author.

First, with only a few small press books of poetry in print, and one remaindered novel, his work was hard to find, let alone buy. The solution was to give it away free on the street.

Secondly, the distribution of his free broadsides and books

were done by enthusiastic Digger volunteers, acting a corps of
unpaid salesman.

And this solved his third problem. His work was so idiosyncratic, it required a new audience, and these Digger
volunteers went out and found it in the Haight. This audience
was one which needed something different from the books put
out by the North Beach literary hierarchy. The young writers I
knew in the Haight enjoyed Richard's plain style, his American
subjects and his fertile, agile imagination. Raving prophets on
amphetamine binges insulting the squares were not new or
interesting. Certainly the jaded existential flavor of the North
Beach literary life was of small interest to the people flooding
the Haight. However, to those runaways, the main publishing
organs of the Beat literature were hip, and since Brautigan had
published in Evergreen Review and City Lights Journal, he was
seen by the street crowd as providing a bridge between their
scene and the older scene.

While critics eventually called his work surrealistic,
Brautigan did not write in the Beat manner of European
surrealism. He considered his writing an offshoot from it. He
once told me that he thought that classic surrealist writing too
easy, especially as it was imitated in North Beach. The name he
had for it was "the mental furniture school," meaning by that
phrase that the writing moved things around on whim, with
no reality to either the changes or the things. He also called it
"of-of" writing, meaning poems in the style of the French
surrealists, such as Breton, citing as an example, hats of lobsters
or newspapers of pianos. This was an odd thing for Richard to
say, since a lot of his early poetry used those exact con-
structions. But then Richard was no critic and he was capable
of uttering condemnatory statements that just as easily could
be levelled against his own writing.

As social critics, the Diggers occasionally reflected Brautigan's positive stance toward America, as a country, and this
attracted fans. One thing that tends to be overlooked about the
hippie scene was it was pro-American, but with a distinctly
western vision of America, one where individualism and
delight in all the senses demanded an anarchistic freedom for

their personal lives. Most important, this western vision issued the refugees of the Haight a license to start their lives over.

This notion concealed an innate right-wing bias too, one which emerged later in the various communes and their ingrown sexism and fascism. This conservatism confounded the reporters from the liberal papers who really wanted to like the Hippie movement if only it would state its political beliefs in a responsible fashion. The Berkeley left-wing, as Charles Perry reported in his book, *The Haight-Ashbury*, also had trouble with the political implications of the Diggers, who often rejected Berkeley's methods and positions on the Vietnam war.

In a similar manner, when Richard found his audience in the Haight and his work began to be bought by more and more people, he was still not considered important by the North Beach establishment of writers. The first big poetry readings and "Be-ins" were held in late 1966, and the stars were North Beach poets. Michael McClure strummed his autoharp, Ginsberg chanted mantras, and Gary Snyder dispensed spiritual and ecological advice. Brautigan was not included even as an opening act. In the events run by the Diggers, Brautigan became a headliner. However, these were more performance events, involving music, street theater and performance art, such as the Invisible Circus at the Glide Church. Once again, they gave him an audience, but didn't improve his literary stock.

The success of *Trout Fishing* and *In Watermelon Sugar* was incomprehensible to most North Beach writers. There was initially a wave of genuine congratulation. As Michael McClure pointed out, "for [the local writers] he was the ugly duckling turned into a swan." In 1968 one writer explained to me that in the early '60s Richard had offered everyone a look at his manuscripts but few had actually bothered to read them. Later on, writers outside California were sure that Brautigan had written his books overnight to cash in on the hippie craze. Actually his first four novels were written before 1967, the year that the national media descended on the flower children.

Two of the obvious bonds between Brautigan and the people living in the Haight were his image and his poverty. His castoff

Navy peacoat, his funky vest decorated with odd buttons and his battered grey hat were part of the uniforms worn around Haight Street. Seeing him at the Diggers Free Public Dinners in the Panhandle only reinforced that image.

For those who read his work, Brautigan's writing used the two cultures that many people there knew—the lower-class life and the dropout California scenes. His charm was that famous cultural icons were pictured with a downhome perspective as, in *Trout Fishing* he imagined Leonardo da Vinci living in America and inventing a fishing lure called "The Last Supper."

The appeal of his work was that Brautigan created a new vision out of the materials at hand, no matter how one-dimensional or banal or fantastic they might seem, no matter how ephemeral or insignificant they might be in accepted cultural terms. This was exactly what people were trying to do with their lives in the Haight, to find a way to start their lives over and make a new order.

If Brautigan's career was pulling out into the passing lane by the late fall of 1966, daily life in the Haight district was about to hit a traffic jam. In his history, *The Haight-Ashbury*, Charles Perry described the situation this way: "In the beginning, new arrivals on Haight Street had not been a problem. Old-timers would teach them the ropes, let them set up as dope dealers or find some other scam, and let them work out their adjustments to an unstructured life. In October you could see a breakdown in this pattern of assimilation. Young runaways weren't finding a way to make a living or even a place to stay. Some of them were sleeping in the park and eating at the Digger Feeds, which had quickly gained a regular clientele of fifty to a hundred. Others were begging on the street."

The visible pattern of drug use changed, too. In the supermarket at the top of Haight Street I once queued up behind a young, conventionally-dressed mother and her child. I happened to look over her shoulder at her errand list. The usual things, from food to appointments, were there, but beside Sunday's slot, in capital letters and underlined three times, was ACID. Among my acquaintances if there was drug use, it had a kind of ritual regularity. The Fillmore weekend dances were favored, but marijuana was about the only drug used on a daily basis, and not many people that I knew even did that. This all changed. On the street, folks stayed stoned every day. They sparechanged for money and became parasites on the increasing flow of younger, more innocent, visitors.

When *Trout Fishing In America* was published in 1967, its patchwork construction, its pastoral lost-paradise themes, and its funky, wacky and innocent voices appeared to mirror events in the Haight. Brautigan's active engagement with the Diggers gave him recognition and a de facto status as Poet Laureate for the street. At last the media had something written and so the novel became an emblem, an explanation, and a target.

The media's attraction to the book caused many literary types to dismiss the novel as another one of Brautigan's topical, quick toss-offs, much like his Digger broadside poem, "Flowers For Those You Love," about where to find the VD clinic. One of the first changes that this reaction to *Trout Fishing* worked on Richard was that he became even more prickly about his prose.

Writing any fiction, from short stories to novels, is hard work, and hard work is never glamorous—while fame always seems so. The two are hard to reconcile privately and, in the public mind, they never do seem to meld together. When the artistic product is comic, its effect becomes absolutely impossible to associate with long hours and endless revisions, since to the audience laughter seems to come so easily. But as any author will tell you, comedy is hard to write. And when comedy comes with a metaphysical tinge, the easiest thing is to ignore that and simply enjoy the laughs. This leads to much sadness among comic authors and results in their common complaint that they are misunderstood.

Another change I noticed in Richard was his attitude toward public readings. He had always been a good reader of his own work, but before his Haight-Ashbury fame started to bloom, he privately regarded reading as preaching to the converted, the small audience of the poetry buffs. He regarded the effort as largely hopeless until his work with the Diggers began to connect him to larger and larger crowds.

With this spur, every reading and every publication became serious business and his apartment showed the change. His long dark hallway no longer displayed other people's art, but was lined with posters for his readings, paste-ups of the covers, mimeo broadsides and letters and artwork from his fans. Each new publication was propped up in a place of honor in front of his aged Mason jars and the rusty mementos of his bleak Northwest childhood. Often I looked at these compositions as if they were offerings to the demons he had fled.

On my visits to San Francisco during 1967, Richard gave me other unpublished manuscripts. One afternoon he handed me *In Watermelon Sugar* to read while he ran an errand. I spent a baffled half an hour trying to figure out what was going on and why he had written it. The novel never has been on my list of favorite Brautigan titles. When he came back, I steered the conversation off my reactions. I talked about his technique and zeroed in on the very spare vocabulary that he used. This prompted him to talk of how he wrote fiction, one of the few times he ever did.

While Richard's method of composition was strict in its own way, it was also eccentric.

"I don't take any notes; I don't work from any outline," he told me. "I don't keep a journal either. Whatever happens to me or any ideas I have sink back in the gunk until the time comes to write. Then, if they come out, fine. I type very fast and I let the first draft come out as fast as it can."

For him there was no halfway about his work—either it arrived or it didn't. He never complained about writer's block, he was either writing or not.

Looking back, the library for the unpublished manuscripts in *The Abortion* and "The Forgotten Works" for neglected books and objects in *In Watermelon Sugar* now seem to reveal his recognition of his precarious literary fate. That he used the negative term gunk for his memory reveals that sometimes he regarded his memory as an impediment to his writing, an obstacle to overcome.

This would explain his schizophrenic behavoir toward his Northwest past—using it for his work but refusing to discuss it otherwise. This is understandable. His imagination was his only sure means of triumphing over his history and all the hurts of growing up as a welfare kid in the Northwest. Memory was simply painful. The art created from memory a joy.

The close scrutiny that he lavished on his prose, sometimes staying up for days revising his novels, rebounded on him in the form of insomnia, a common complaint among writers. I thought that Richard's overactive imagination and blitzkrieg work habits were the cause, but, after he died, his daughter Ianthe told me that his mother abandoned him and his younger sister in a hotel in Great Falls, Montana. Richard was nine years old and he was left as the sole support of his sister. They lived on food supplied by a sympathetic cook in the hotel. Brautigan told his daughter that he couldn't sleep at night, waiting for his mother to return, and that he had suffered from chronic sleeplessness ever since that time.

Another aspect of this story strikes me. All through Brautigan's work, doors constantly appear, sometimes as images of separation, but most often as symbols for changes in life. I wondered if those days and nights of staring at a hotel door, waiting for his mother to return, perhaps transformed doors into a personal fetish.

This hands-off attitude toward his past was also another one of Richard's ties to the psychedelic generation: the insistence on the present, the here and now. One of the codes in the Haight was that one never asked anyone what they used to do, or why they were there, or where they came from. In his fiction, Richard mirrored this penchant for self-creation among the pyschedelic generation and versions of it are found in his work. This passage from *In Watermelon Sugar* became a backpocket favorite with the kids in the Haight-Ashbury.

I guess you are kind of curious as to who I am, but I am one of those who do not have a regular name. My name depends on you. Just call me whatever is in your mind.

If you are thinking about something that happened a

long time ago: Somebody asked you a question and
you did not know the answer.
   That is my name.
   Perhaps it was raining very hard.
   That is my name.
   Or somebody wanted you to do something. You did
it. Then they told you what you did was wrong—
"Sorry for the mistake,"—and you had to do something
else.
   That is my name.

Unlike most of the Haight-Ashbury psychedelic regulars,
Brautigan relied on his imagination to transform reality. Sometimes when an imaginative view of mundane reality is insisted
on, this worked to the detriment of his material. His trans-
formations seemed forced, or unearned. His imagination relied
too much on cleverness and whimsy only acted as a distraction
to the reader from the matter at hand. His poetry often suffered
from this. Sometimes his short impressionistic fiction did too,
as in this paragraph from "Sand Castles" from *Revenge of the
Lawn*:

   Hawks circle in the sky like the lost springs of old
   railroad watches looking for correct protein wandering
   somewhere below to swoop down upon and devour
   chronologically.

On a personal level, *In Watermelon Sugar* later seemed to me a
book Richard wrote in reaction to his divorce from his first wife,
Virginia Adler. When they fell in love, he was living in a
flophouse and working as a Western Union messenger. More
sophisticated and literate than he was, she supported his
writing habit via secretarial jobs. After the birth of Ianthe, they
saved enough for an idyllic trip to Idaho during 1961. "We'd
camp beside the streams, and Richard would get out his old
portable typewriter and a card table. That's when he began to
write *Trout Fishing in America*." This pastoral ended on their
return to San Francisco. Richard had the habit of abandoning

her at night to hang out in North Beach. Tired of being left with
the baby, Virginia had an affair with one of Brautigan's friends
and moved with him to Salt Lake City. This devastated
Richard. *In Watermelon Sugar* was written shortly after this
breakup. Even with its fairy tale setting, this novel never struck
me as childish. With a limited vocabulary and its insistence on
living in the present, despite betrayals, the narrative functions
as a kind of coda about personal loss, and about the need to
leave things and relationships in "The Forgotten Works."

Richard was quite vain about his imagination. It was his
main asset, so he was often scornful of different powers of
mind. After his first East Coast reading tour, he told how he'd
been to Harvard and other Ivy League colleges and now he
was "so bored with people who are only smart."

He was joking, of course, but in another sense he was
serious. He regarded intellectual prowess as inferior to the
imagination. He also feared memory as a crippling power and
for that reason he regarded memory also as an inferior intellectual faculty. Thorton Wilder once commented that intellect is
not forged from suffering. Intellectual prowess is a reaction to it,
a way, as Wilder says, "to explain to yourself why you suffer."
It is clear in his work that Brautigan felt creative imagination is
born of suffering and when art is alive enough to endure, it can
triumph over suffering. As he wrote of his poverty-stricken
childhood friend, The Kool-Aid Wino: "He created his own
Kool-Aid reality and was able to illuminate himself by it."

However, Richard didn't scorn the intellectual discipline of
editing. Once the initial pellmell draft of a work was done, then
he worked long days on editing his prose. He was rather
ferocious about revision. He would often call me up during
these editing sprees, sometimes late at night, and read me a
sentence. His idiosyncratic tic was to read only one.

"What do you think of this?" he'd say, and read it again.
"What do you think?"

The sentence was invariably straightforward and without
many complications. I never knew what he thought was wrong
with it. I can't remember when I was of any use to him on a
particular sentence. I'd ask him to read the other sentences

before or after the one that bothered him, but he never would. He'd obsessively reread the same sentence over and over, never able to articulate what it was that was bothering him. Finally I'd say that I thought it was fine. He'd agree, but dubiously, and hang up. Perhaps an hour later, he'd call back and read another sentence and ask me if that sounded right. This could go on for a few days, and then he would call up, apologize profusely for troubling me, and invite me out to dinner as payment.

Although I never could discover what bothered him about those sentences, whenever I confined my comments to the feelings that arose from them, he paid close attention to what I said. These impressions were more valuable to him than specifics. I later decided he was using me as a gauge for the emotional tones because he always enjoyed the emotional qualities of my writing.

He never called me about punctuation or grammar. I suspected that, given Richard's precise cast of mind, if he didn't rely on himself, he had some other friend to call on for his commas and tenses.

This penchant was a curious constant about Richard in the early years. Although he asked for advice, he seemed incapable of taking it—or love for that matter—except on the rare occasions when those channels were open for him. The burden was on his friends to accept whatever he gave.

Although he lived on an emotional one-way street for most of his life, he was pleased when someone found imaginative ways for verbal feedback. Usually these comments had to be spontaneous—any other praise seemed like statues to Richard, laborious monuments to past moments. He saw the world as filled with monuments to dead imagination, and he was contemptuous of such. This attitude can be found in all his work (along with a lot of statuary). What he valued were the moments when imagination blazed and the world was vivid.

His inability to feel empathy for those who recognized their own lack of imagination, but worshipped it in others was a curious blind spot with him. This trait created difficulties for his daily life when the media turned him into a breathing statue for the myth of the Haight-Ashbury. And, in the same ironical way, Brautigan's novels became an emblem for a way of life which was already dead by 1968 when his writing began to sell.

In early 1967 the Diggers tried to showcase their version of what the Haight-Ashbury should be doing. At the Glide Memorial Church in San Francisco's Tenderloin they held what they titled The Invisible Circus—the Right of Spring. In true Digger fashion, they gave it alternate titles, "It's Yours" and "It's Here," but tenatively set the date for Friday, February 24. According to Charles Perry, this event was in reaction to the first Be-In held in January, which the Diggers criticized heavily. "In a way [the Invisible Circus] was a vision of what the Be-In ought to have been," Charles Perry noted. "Not a passive stroll around the speakers' platform but a participatory event. Not in the park but downtown in the gritty Tenderloin. Not healthful, peaceful and decorous but smutty, rebellious and possibly dangerous. Not four hours in the afternoon but seventy-two hours of nonstop happenings."

The Diggers tried this also because their other projects had fallen on hard times. Their free dinners in the Panhandle were strained to the limit by the numbers of transients. Their store, the Free Frame of Reference, had been padlocked shut by the authorities as a public nuisance. The Diggers needed a new venue and The Invisible Circus was going to show people how things should be done.

While Richard had continued to work with the Diggers, by January of 1967 his enthusiasm flagged. He recognized the situation in the Haight for what it was: media-fed chaos with middle-class runaways flooding the streets. After New Year's, he became very bitter. "The Haight—that's where people come from all across the country to sit in their own shit on a doorstep."

During planning of The Invisible Circus, Brautigan's interest revived. He was put in charge of the Diggers' Gestetner mimeos and assigned a room at the Glide Church. Use of the equipment was free. Anyone who wanted to print something was given help in typesetting and running off copies of whatever they wished. With his usual hyperbole, Richard dubbed this motley collection of printing machinery The John Dillinger Computer Complex, in recognition of its supposedly outlaw status. Because the alternative newspapers were still few, and those few were frequently busted and harassed, unofficial news which was not "co-opted by the established powers" seemed glamorously rebellious.

The concept of a populist anti-media media reflected the larger street theater bias of the Invisible Circus. Planning was minimal. Earlier in the week, the word went out in the Haight-Ashbury that if there was something that you always wanted to do, but never had a room to do it in, come to the Invisible Circus at eight o'clock and you could do it. Richard claimed that the location of the happening was kept secret until the very last minute.

True to this concept, Brautigan called me in Monterey and asked me to put my van at the Diggers' disposal, but he refused to say why or for what. "Just come," he ordered. "You won't want to miss it."

On Thursday I drove up and all Friday morning I helped truck spare mimeo machines, donated paper, stencils and other supplies to the Glide. Others lugged in shredded plastic and filled a hallway with it. Someone else turned an office into a sewing room. As the starting time of 8:00 drew near, all sorts of rumors arose, from a guest appearance of Big Brother and the Holding Company to a "Slo-Mo Destruction Derby" in the parking lot with junker cars. What actually happened was much more random, lunatic and scary than any of the rumors. Ironically, it turned out exactly like the Haight-Ashbury. What started as an improvised, multi-layered theater experience was soon overrun by a lemming tide of people, most of whom were looney.

This exercise in anarchy provided Richard with one of his favorite stories. Apparently, some people decided that they always wanted to run a coffee shop, and so they took over a long conference room and dispensed coffee. Theoretically, the rooms were available only for a certain number of hours to each group. This happened at first, but the crush got so bad that no one could get things out, let alone new stuff in. Richard delighted in telling how one change of room ownership was effected. Late that night, when the madness was at its height, Brautigan was sitting in the coffee shop with a member of the church board. Both men were exhausted, drinking coffee, and too tired to do any more than ignore the pornographic film that someone else was showing on a bedsheet draped over the far end of the room.

"The movie was boring, the people were ugly, and what they were doing was ugly. The two of us drank our coffee and discussed how the craziness was going to end," Richard related. "That was when I noticed that the coffee shop people were packing up their goods and leaving. Just as they left, and when the porno movie ended, the sheet split and out came two strippers with a band blasting out bump and grind music behind them." Richard said the church member told him that was it, he was abandoning ship.

Up in the John Dillinger Computer Complex, things weren't much better. All the machines but one had broken-down, largely due to inexperienced operators, but also from metal fatigue. The only running mimeo was jealously hoarded by a speed freak who was busy cranking out gibberish, rumors and transcripts of local Tenderloin bar talk in the form of an hourly newsletter. These communiques were rushed out so quickly that often the ink hadn't dried and the halls were soon carpeted with the mushed remains.

At twelve that night Richard was supposed to read in the sanctuary. Earlier in the day, he had sent someone out to Point Reyes to get a bucket of oysters. When I asked, he acted mysterious about what connection the oysters had to his reading. As it turned out, the oysters didn't have much to do with the event at all. By twelve that night, the crush in the building was tidal. Not only did the entire Haight-Ashbury seem to be there, so were Tenderloin winos, sailors on leave, escaped mental patients, cruising transvestites, karmic basket cases, tourists and local street trade. When the Diggers tried to feed everyone at eleven o'clock, the entire population tried to cram themselves into the dining hall. Gridlock occurred in all the hallways. During the night I got trapped in one room after another because there were so many bodies passing by outside that it looked like a subway train of human flesh. This was not fun.

In the hallway filled with shredded plastic someone threw the light switch and a group grope ensued. This might have been a result of the waiting line to get into the Bridal Chamber. Some enterprising erotic philantropists had set up a sensory bedchamber there, with feathers, furs, balloons, incense, music and all manner of sexual aids and redubbed it the Fuck Room. They were letting couples in for twenty minute workouts. Apparently the long queue for the Bridal Chamber had become impatient and staged a takeover of the shredded plastic corridor.

Around midnight Richard was scheduled to read, but when he stepped up to the altar, he looked out over chaos. The sanctuary was smoky and dim from candles, cigarettes, incense and dope. LSD had been handed out earlier, and the people were loud, loaded and lunatic. The mob quieted for a second when they saw Brautigan, perhaps out of respect for his status or just out of curiosity. But when he announced that he was dedicating his reading to oysters and put the pail on the altar, that was the last that could be heard. The sanctuary returned to bedlam as usual.

If there was a further reason for this gesture, or even a poem to commemorate it, I never knew what it was. The crowd noise drowned him out. Brautigan tried to read some poems, but then gave up. Even with a PA system, no one could hear him.

After less than eight hours, what was planned as a three day festival was closed down by the church officials at four in the morning. As the head of the John Dillinger Computer Complex, Richard was in the final meeting that dissolved the Invisible Circus.

"Everything had gotten so crazy by that time," he reported the next day, "that none of the church members were even mentioning what was going on in the Bridal Chamber any more. One of the Diggers had selected some speed freak as his representative. Between each speech by the church members, this guy would spew out a rap. It was like counterpoint. Everyone was trying to figure out some way to get the mob out of the church without calling the police and starting a riot."

Richard reported that one board member was in a trance. He kept repeating over and over, "The one thing we agreed on was no naked bodies on the altar, and what did we get? *Naked bodies on the altar."*

III. Monterey Pop, 1967

n April 1967 my place in the mortal chain became all too evident. I became a father at age twenty-three when my daughter Persephone was born. Twelve days later, my father died of a heart attack. It seemed that I should assume more responsibility, but the times were not conducive to long-range planning. I had to provide for my family, yet I was determined to be a writer.

After Persephone was born, we moved into a large, long, drafty, lovely old house in Pacific Grove, with a wall of windows overlooking the bay. This marvelous old shack rented for $50 a month and had enough spare rooms to put up my San Francisco friends. So they came and stayed and cheerfully disrupted what writing schedule I had built up over the winter. While I still traveled up to the city, school and baby business kept me home more often than not.

A Haight-Ashbury reunion for some of my old friends occurred, though, the weekend of the Monterey Pop Festival, June 16. Monterey Pop was the first rock festival. Very impromptu, it functioned without any of the rent-a-cops and tight security that would characterize future rock events.

Students at the Monterey community college were offered jobs there, so I signed on as a security guard for the front gate. In the tempting chaos of the festival, though, this makeshift staff soon disintegrated. Many of students split, either because they couldn't handle the pressure, or they wanted to get loaded and dance the night away.

The fellow I was paired with, Ken, managed to stick around until Saturday. A philosophy major, Ken was a straight kid from the suburbs and had never even been to the Haight-Ashbury. For him the scene was a revelation. He was so innocent that he only vaguely understood my warning against taking any drink or food offered him. But the concert-goers looked and acted so weird that he heeded my advice. Once he found out that I had majored in philosophy at the University of Washington, he became more interested in passing time by talking about Bishop Berkeley and David Hume than listening to rock and roll.

Because of our sobriety, Ken and I were upgraded to being guards at the south backstage door on Saturday morning. Although I had been to the Fillmore dances, I had never been behind the scenes, so this gave me my first close look at rock musicians and their entourages, including groupies.

Once we pulled backstage duty, there was no slack time. We got hit on every second by someone. Everyone had to get backstage. Under these pressures, Ken soon got into trouble. While I was running an errand to the hashish den that was called the performers' lounge, two groupies hit on Ken and promised him anything. He was so tired and hungry that he agreed to let them backstage if they brought him some food. When I returned, Ken was eating two hamburgers. I assumed he'd slipped away somehow and bought them himself. I resumed my post at the bottom of the stairs and Ken manned the door.

The routine was that I'd play hard cop, discourage as many as I could, and pass up to Ken any really obnoxious people. He spoke very softly and had a straight, no-nonsense manner that sometimes worked. We'd been given a list of the groups with strict instructions that anyone not connected to the afternoon concert was to be refused backstage access.

The Beach Boys were not on that list, so when their drummer demanded entrance, I said no. The Beach Boy nodded, acted as if I had said yes, and bounded up the stairs to Ken. As I followed him up, a familar smell of old Mexico drifted out of the large, half-full Safeway shopping bag he was holding. When

Ken didn't open the door, the Beach Boy leaned over and whispered, "Got the stuff. Lemme in."

Ken was staring off into the trees and smiling. The Beach Boy waited, his eyes fixed on the door. "They're waiting," the Beach Boy explained.

Now, this bag had clearly turned the Beach Boy into an exception to our strict orders, and I said to Ken to let him backstage.

Ken ignored me, turned to the Beach Boy and crooned juicily, "Letcha in, if ya tell me why Bishop Berkeley negated the motorcar."

The Beach Boy continued to stare at the door. "Got the stuff," he repeated again. "Lemme in."

Ken coyly wagged his finger at him. "First ya gotta tell me why Bishop Berkeley negated the motor car! It's easy," he hinted.

The Beach Boy noticed that the door wasn't opening. He looked over at Ken, seeing him for the first time.

Ken smiled reassuringly. "So why did Bishop Berkeley negate the motor car?" Ken prompted him again. "Why? Because . . . come on, you know . . . because . . ."

"Good news!" the Beach Boy snarled, opening the bag and pushing it up for Ken to see.

Ken didn't even look in, he was thinking so hard about what the Beach Boy said. A stunned look swept over Ken's face as he realized the absolute profoundity of the Beach Boy's answer to why Bishop Berkeley negated the motorcar.

"Good news! Oh! Oh yeah!" he breathed. "Good news. Wow, that's right! That's why! Good news! Yeah, you got it right!"

"Right this way," I said, gently pushing Ken aside and opening the door. The Beach Boy disappeared inside to service the mob of musicians there.

Shortly after that, I spotted a friend in the crowd and sent Ken home with him, explaining that he was a casualty of the event. Ken recovered with no ill effects, but other scenes there were not so pleasant.

On Sunday afternoon, the Ravi Shankar concert exhausted my ability to say no. Before his show was to start, more people were lounging in the backstage area than in front of it. To perserve his serenity for his music, Shankar requested that the stage be cleared and that no one be allowed backstage during his set. Two of his aides were positioned inside the stage doors to enforce this.

My duty was to turn away rock stars, their managers and anyone else, and I got mountains of crap. One entourage from a Los Angeles band was particularly trying. They were called the No-Names on the program, because a title hadn't been found for their group yet. Their anonymous status seemed to exacerbate their insecurities. Ravi was a personal friend, of course, and they were confident that he wanted them close by. Screaming, threats and hissy fits were showered on me. Some of the Who entourage showed up and they were not used to being told no. Very quickly the situation turned loud, messy and stupid.

Since, if anyone got really ugly, I was instructed to turn them over to one of Shankar's aides inside the back door, I did so immediately. Motioning for one ego to step up at a time, I'd knock, the aide would stick his head out, say no, and duck back in. Eventually things got really raucous. The aide had to step out and defuse the situation with his calm and reasonable explanations of Ravi's need for a serene backstage. Helped by the exaggerated respect that was then given to the mystic East, this fellow succeeded in soothing and sending away the giant egos. But it was touch and go.

That afternoon was my first exposure to the arrogance that fame confers. Although I had had experience talking someone down from a drug-induced megalomania, only a drug is supporting the delusion. In the case of fame, the cast of supporting characters and situations are usually much larger, much stronger and more tenacious. Eliminating a drug from someone's system can be done, but fame is a much more stubborn narcotic.

Shortly after the Festival, I returned to San Francisco for a visit and got a good look at what Brautigan's onrushing fame was providing. The first thing I noticed was that his apartment had been completely cleaned from front to back. Fresh surplus parachutes hung over the long dark entrance. For the first time in my memory the floor had been washed. A school of Brautigan's trademark smiling trout had been painted all the way down the hallway and into his funky living room. A happy trout even swam across his toilet seat.

While we were at his house, one lovely woman of about eighteen kept us company and then left. We went out to dinner where a second girl, equally willowy and young, joined us. After dinner we left her, took a cab to the Fillmore Auditorium where a blonde woman and three complimentary tickets for an Eric Burdon, Steve Miller and Chuck Berry concert were waiting. Just about everything about this night amazed me, from the cab ride to the trio of literary groupies to the comps. In Monterey I had no idea how quickly *Trout Fishing In America* had given Brautigan local fame.

While literary groupies weren't uncommon, they usually came one at a time. What astounded me was our comp tickets and his new fans. Brautigan had never shown much interest in rock before, and during the concert he paid no attention to the music. He strolled around and collected accolades from the kids. Some shied away and simply gaped, as if they didn't dare approach. This treatment reminded me of Monterey, where Roger Daltry and Michelle Philips had paraded around in extremely expensive silk clothes, trailed by adoring fans. While the comps were a clear indication that Brautigan's reputation had outgrown literary boundaries, the teenagers idolizing him weren't Haight Street runaways, but middle-class kids with enough money for concerts. When I returned to Monterey, I wrote to a friend, "Richard's getting laid by a bevy of 18-year olds." But that was only a convenient shorthand symbol for the fame he'd come into. The evening had seemed unreal, as if I were walking with a rock star who was dressed like funky old Richard.

With Michael McClure, ca. 1975.

San Francisco snapshots. RB and Virginia on back porch, RB and Virginia (pregnant), and RB with Ianthe, September 1962.

Two snapshots taken on the U.C. Santa Barbara campus in February 1967.

Left: RB with Andy Hoyem (center) and unidentified student.

Below: RB with Jack Shoemaker (left), Basil Bunting, Andy Hoyem (seated), and Mairia Bunting. (Standing woman unidentified.)

IV. Fame, 1967-1974

S udden fame creates a vacuum around a person. Much gets siphoned out of a person's life as other things rush in. When fame befalls a friend, things most familiar are hidden from the public while traits quite strange to your experience are so blown up, they seem to become that friend. The dangers of such a process are well rehearsed in the popular biographies of movie actors where they become their roles. For writers, popular acclaim creates a more elemental hazard: addiction to personal recognition.

A writer's job is necessarily lonely, because normally only one person writes a book. Public gratifications arrive long after the writing is done. Seeing an author's back cover photograph is often the closest that people come to their favorites. Brautigan put his photographs on the front of his books and actively courted public recognition. After all, that strategy had worked for him in the Haight, rescuing his career. As Becky Fonda recalled, during the heady years that Richard was famous, taking a walk with him in San Francisco was apt to draw a crowd. "Richard was really undone by fame," she said. "He couldn't believe what was happening to him. [Once] we had to run for cover into Peggy's Used Clothing Store because he was just being mobbed."

An interesting sidelight of Brautigan's fame is that his books had no heroes, other than the first person narrators. Jack Kerouac cast Dean Moriarty as Neal Cassady and Japhy Ryder as Gary Snyder for his heroes, and Ken Kesey invented the

63

Coyote trickster, cuckoo Murphy. But Brautigan presented versions only of himself in his early books. The fans thought they were buying Brautigan when they bought his books. Unfortunately, he invested in this fallacy, too, and put his face, girlfriends and even his phone number on the covers of his work.

On a radio broadcast after his death, his close friend Ron Loewinsohn commented that public recognition became like a drug to Brautigan. Even though Richard admitted to friends that this was necessarily fleeting, emotionally he came to expect it.

In his book, *Demon Box*, Ken Kesey recalled his own brush with this addiction to fame during the 1960s.

I was happy to be getting out of the U.S. That book about me and my Kool Aid cronies had just come out and I felt the hot beam of the spotlight on me. It burned like a big ultraviolet eye. The voltage generated by all this attention scared me a little and titillated me a lot, and I needed a breather from it before I became an addict, or a casualty. Stand in this spotlight, feel this eye pass over you. You never forget it. You are suddenly changed, lifted, singled out, elevated and alone, above any of your bush-league frets of stage fright, nagging scruples, etc. Self-consciousness and irresolution melt in this beam's blast. Grace and power surge in to take their place. Banging speed is the only thing even close. Drowsing protoplasm snaps instantly to Bruce Lee perfection—enter the dragon. But there's the scaly rub, right? Because you go around to the other end of that eye and look through at the star shining there so elevated, you see that this adoring telescope has crosshairs built in it. . . .

For a writer, the intoxication of this moment seems even more exhilarating and disorienting than for, say, an actor, since a product—a book or play or movie—stands between himself and his public. Stepping out from behind that shield has to be such a risk and such a rush. One of the most revealing accounts of Brautigan becoming the hero of his books was remembered by the writer Bobbie Louise Hawkins:

> The first trip Richard ever made east, he was standing in Harvard Square, and up Mass. Ave there comes a parade in the very front row of which are four young women. The middle two are carrying a gigantic papier-mâché trout, and the outside two are carrying poles with a banner between them reading, *Trout Fishing In America*. The parade was for some school in Cambridge named for the book, and Richard's reaction was sheer ecstasy and delight. Once Richard was recognized, he joined the parade. I don't think he had any awareness of how damaging celebrity might be.

Richard removed that barrier between his work and himself. He became a symbol and his writing merely an accoutrement of that symbol. He joined the parade. And, Banging speed is the only thing even close.

Richard's own account of his first perception of his oncoming reknown was realistic and commonplace. He told me that he knew he was going to be famous the day he walked into his neighborhood Chinese grocery and saw that the teenage girl at the cash register was reading *Trout Fishing In America*. Although he had shopped there for years, he said there was no way that he could have ever convinced her to buy one of his novels.

This was Richard's funny off-angle admission that his fame was no longer in his hands, that his writing was now played with by bigger forces than he could control. But rather than be frightened by this, he professed delight. The randomness of celebrity brought out the latent macho side of him, the side that pretended that he could handle rough stuff, take the blows that fate might offer.

When I transferred to San Francisco State in January of 1968, I found my family a one-bedroom flat in the Richmond district and I started the commute to the campus. We were paying $115 a month rent while living on a total budget of $145 a month, supplemented with food stamps. Lani learned to cook Chinese food, using the cheap vegetable markets on Clement Street, and soon we were involuntary vegetarians, submitting to the joys of bok choy and more bok choy. Whenever we could afford hamburger, our main meat dish was chili. I soon weighed 190 pounds, my weight as a high school junior.

For extra money, I tried to find work as a moving man when I could take time from school, but time was scarce. I was carrying eighteen hours, five English classes and one Political Science, writing a paper a week in an attempt to finish my BA by the summer. I'd been accepted as a graduate student for the fall term 1968, given a TA's job and enough student aid for my family to exist on, so I was determined to graduate.

The money we saved in Monterey was soon exhausted. Eventually I had to sell my truck and to borrow from my mother. Lani took part-time work in the afternoons, while I stayed with my daughter and wrote papers. With this schedule, I saw Brautigan infrequently and hardly ever got over to Haight Street. When we did meet, news of his rising acclaim dominated our conversation. I remember more than once having a twinge of envy over his good luck, yet I was genuinely glad for him. Certainly he was both aware of my situation and my feelings. One day, after I had worked for Lyons moving company and had a little cash, I met him for a quick afternoon drink. This soon snowballed into a party at a restaurant, and then the bill arrived. My share was more than my food budget for the month.

Richard saw the look on my face. "This was my scene," he said and he pocketed the check. "You wouldn't have done this otherwise."

His sudden popularity was like a new toy. His egocentric fascination seemed forgiveable after his years of poverty and neglect. But to others it was grating, especially to the revolutionaries of the Haight. After all, he hadn't written four novels in five years so he could discuss other people's plans for radical social change, but this was not considered. Friends, like the

Digger Peter Berg, found his continual fascination with fame distasteful.

> Richard would talk about how many books he sold last week. It was constant, to the point where that was his only conversation, and I started calling him Richard Career. That was the end of our relationship.

By 1968, Brautigan's three books from Four Seasons were selling well, but only in small press terms. While not rich, he no longer had to scuffle for rent and food and he was able to pay child support for his daughter. He found his local success to be deliciously ironic, because New York publishers were looking around the Haight-Ashbury for what one editor called "the Catch-22 of the hippies." When Brautigan's works eventually were sold to Delacorte, these trade paperbacks quickly became the media symbols for the Haight-Ashbury. The ride to best-seller status was fast and heady. In two years' time, Brautigan went from handing out free mimeo broadsides to selling a hundred thousand books. A profile of him ran in *Life* magazine, and his stories appeared in national publications like *Rolling Stone* and *Esquire.*

If Richard seemed animated when he was working with the Diggers, after his career took off he became comically harried and hysterical. I remember stopping by his flat in 1968 and he spent almost the entire time talking on the phone about upcoming publications and readings. While he couldn't afford an answering service, he did have an on-off toggle switch installed on his phone. Yet Richard wasn't so involved that he couldn't joke about his fame. As we were leaving for dinner, he stopped by the phone. "Mistah Brautigan," he said in his best deadpan style, flipping the switch off, "he dead."

The common dichotomies in a famous writer's life are usually two: the difference between the work and the public image of the work, and the difference between the writer and his public image. These disparities make Brautigan's case most interesting.

To Richard's friends, fame's melding of him into his public, front-cover persona was ironic. In the public eye, he became a spokesman for a way of life that was certainly connected to his Digger days and giveaway poetry broadsides, but had few real connections with his first four books of fiction, which were written before 1967. Essentially a loner, he was ballyhooed as the head of a communal generation, stereotyped as the gentle hippie—an image his poems supported but which his novels, with their bleak and elegiaic sense of human relationships, did not.

The appeal of his writing to the young people in 1968 came from the same source as his weakness in life: an ability to ignore common sense and concentrate on the uncommon sense which his mind was constantly stewing up. If it is true that the brain contains layers of filters for experience, then Brautigan's lacked some, for he could see things in primal ways—his work's major connection to the psychedelic generation.

When he wrote in *Trout Fishing* that a mother's nagging voice was "filled with sand and string," it made sense to kids who were listening to the Beatle's Eleanor Rigby keeping her face in a jar by the door or Bob Dylan's conductor who "smoked my eyelids and punched my cigarette." And, for people who were being busted down to point zero by LSD, Richard's use of simple and direct American speech was a natural. Those little sentences were easy to read when ripped.

While the cover images of Brautigan personified pothead hippies, the private person did not. As far as I could find out, Brautigan never took psychedelic drugs. Ianthe claimed he was afraid of them and feared they would destroy his creativity. According to his friend, photographer Erik Weber, Richard occasionally smoked pot up until 1967. By early 1968, he had quit even social pot smoking, largely because he dreaded being busted by a celebrity-seeking cop, an event not unknown in California. I never saw him smoke any. I saw him pointedly refuse a joint more than once, saying that he preferred wine or whiskey.

National attention to his work became the plus side of fame. His confidence bloomed, and during 1968 he wrote his best short stories which appeared in *Rolling Stone* early in 1969 and were published later in *Revenge of the Lawn*. Many of these stories were about his childhood. Fame freed him to write about those unhappy times. In the flurry of publicity about his comic writing, this undercurrent went unremarked since it was unfashionable. Problems were caused when his fans believed his public image was reflected inside his books. What got ignored was Brautigan's preoccupation with death, destruction and the fragility of human relationships.

In a radio interview, Don Carpenter talked about how rabid fans warped Brautigan's public image and the problems this public acclaim caused him. "Brautigan was constantly running into readers who said, 'I love you, and let's see, there's you, and Dostoevsky, and Rod McKuen. Those are my three favorite writers.' When a writer gets readers who don't understand his work, he doesn't want those readers. But you've got them, they've paid for your book, and you want their money. There's a contradiction. Then when they go away, again there's a contradictory feeling. Goodbye and good riddance, but leave your money. These contradictions really bothered Brautigan."

It was natural that Brautigan wanted to present the best side of himself to the public, the happy and loving and intensely funny person his friends found so endearing. The cover photographs of himself and his girlfriends Marcia, Valerie, Cheri, and Victoria were calculated to provide that effect. But to understand Brautigan's life, his escape from his unhappy and haunted Northwest childhood is as essential as is his inability to exorcize the demons of lacklove and isolation. To shed his childhood history and his isolated adult life, his private self created fictional, alternate worlds that sustained him. The fictions found an audience, but one which only fitfully understood them.

Beyond the creature comforts of food, drink, and shelter, Richard was too much an outsider ever to trust societal values. Even after his new-found fame provided avenues to so many of society's rewards for success, he found ways of symbolizing his status as loner. Money he habitually scorned as unimportant, and he was suspicious of the joys of the nuclear family, hearth and two-car garage.

His dark vision of society was inspired in part by his Northwest upbringing. For most of his childhood he was an outcast—the weirdo on welfare, the goofy kid whose brain, as novelist Tom McGuane has so aptly said, "was his only toy."

Brautigan told an anecdote once, illustrating his attitude toward the rewards of society. During his junior high school years, Richard claimed he was a terror. He recalled slicing the bottoms of dog food sacks with razor blades in stores, carefully putting them back on the shelves, and then waiting for shoppers to pick them up. He also caused his teachers a lot of trouble with his pranks. Out of boredom with his screwing off, one day he decided to do everything right. For a semester he got straight As, astonishing his teacher. But he abandoned the experiment, because he couldn't find any reason to continue. The rewards weren't worth the trouble. As far as he could tell, doing things right only led to the bondage of always doing things right according to other people's standards.

When Richard assigned worth, he did it totally. People were in or out, actions good or bad, things terrible or terrific. If someone crossed Richard, he rejected them. Forgiveness was never one of his strong suits. In some crucial ways, Richard remained an adolescent all his life. And, like a teenager who lets himself be dominated by his emotions, he could be remarkably blind to his own contradictions.

One day, when we were on Clement Street to do some food shopping, he stopped at a record store and pointed at the album covers.

"Another rock star posing on the front of his record, I'm so tired of that."

He was completely oblivious to his own book covers in the window of the bookstore next door, prominently displaying him and his girlfriends.

Of course, Brautigan could be as starstruck as any writer. He certainly understood the money available if one could get a song credit on a record album. When I first returned to San Francisco in early 1968, his books were just starting to sell out in editions of 5,000. He had about three hundred a month income then and so he was still hustling. He commandeered my 1951 Chevy truck to take some poems over to Janis Joplin. She had successfully collaborated with Michael McClure on the song "Oh Lord, Won't You Buy Me A Mercedes Benz" and Richard claimed that she wanted to sing some of his lyrics on her next album.

I was rather skeptical about this. Richard's poetry lacked rhyme or any regular meter, and Joplin's talent seemed a bit coarse for Richard's delicate verse. I remained curious enough to truck him over to Joplin's flat, but I didn't voice any of my doubts. He was quite high about this chance and did not want to hear any "yeah buts" from me.

As it turned out, Janis was not in, but two of her tough, leather-clad girlfriends were. One took his two poems with thinly veiled contempt and showed us the door.

As he handed the poems over, though, I saw their titles and later located them in his work. After that, whenever I came across "The Horse That Had A Flat Tire" and "She Sleeps This Very Evening In Greenbrook Castle," I always had a good laugh, imagining Janis belting out those two.

> "She sleeps this very eveeeee-ning in Greenbuh-buh-brook Castle, babeee!"

What I remember about Brautigan between the fall of 1968 to the fall of 1970 resembles a random slide show, the memories blurred and chaotic, with little continuity. September 1968 was supposed to have begun a period of security for me. From being a grad student at San Francisco State, I had a regular income for the first time in years, tiny as it was. I also had my own writing room in our new apartment. But two things occurred that destroyed this optimism.

First, the students rioted. I was caught in a day-by-day attempt to survive. Beatings were common, paranoia rampant, and my hours there were a blur. Secondly, because of our daughter and my work, we needed a larger flat and moved into the Haight-Ashbury district. We had no idea how dangerous daily life had become when we rented an apartment at 1918 Oak Street. One of our friends had a printing shop in the Haight and Lani and I had heard a few stories of bad scenes, but we weren't prepared for life in Dodge City. Gunshots or loud fights flared up nearly every night. People were sometimes mugged and beaten in our doorway. Across the street gangs roamed the Panhandle. Soon we never left our apartment after dark. During the day Lani carried our daughter in a backpack and she once had a near-miss with a psychotic Vietnam war vet. We lived in a war zone and from there I commuted to a riot.

We couldn't afford another move, so we tried to cope. I got in the habit of leaving our flat with only change for the bus, in case I got mugged. I also carried a transistor radio for warnings of any violence in progress, so I could pick a safe entrance to the school.

Luckily, Lani received a small inheritance that winter. We left California for England. My writing went badly as I was undergoing a slow nervous breakdown occasioned by my withdrawal from the battle zones. My journal for 1969 is a hodge-podge of verbal flicks of poetry, with almost no daily information, as if any attempt at chronology was beyond me. Pasted in the back, however, are Brautigan's short stories from the *Rolling Stone.* His fiction was one of my few connections to San Francisco.

We then moved to Bellingham, Washington, where I resumed graduate work at Western Washington State. While there, I helped arrange a reading for Brautigan and Michael McClure. Happy and ebullient, Richard was glowing with confidence. He showed me proofs for *Revenge of the Lawn* and told me of the lucrative deal he'd recently signed with Simon & Schuster. From other friends in San Francisco, I had heard rumblings of displeasure. The remarkable sales of Brautigan's Delacorte Press books had created a backwash of envy and jealousy among the writers there.

In the fall of 1970 we returned to Monterey. I had no money and few prospects. While in Bellingham I finished a draft of my novel, *Gush.* With Brautigan's help, the manuscript circulated, but there were no takers. I returned to the gardening business, building up a clientele of afternoon customers, saving mornings for writing. Whenever I traveled to San Francisco during the early 1970s, I would plan a day with Richard, and he could fill me in on his latest good news. By then the critical reception for his work, never overwhelmingly positive in the beginning, had soured considerably. Maintaining his privacy had become a bigger problem. Requests for personal appearances were continual and his publishers wanted him on talk shows to promote his books. But Richard realized his books sold without that kind of publicity. So he didn't bother. Some people thought it arrogant because he never explained why; he simply refused. His privacy was constantly invaded. He loved his fame, and while he courted the public by displaying himself prominently at Enrico's, he complained when his private life—and especially his past—was investigated. It was pointless to tell him he couldn't have it both ways.

During 1969 a self-appointed biographer trailed Brautigan relentlessly. The pest sent for his birth certificate from Tacoma and one morning, when Richard opened the door, the fellow held the document in front of his face as if it were a passport to his life.

"Now will you let me write your bio?" the man said, stepping into the flat.

Richard turned the man around and escorted him out. Later he wrote a poem about this would-be biographer, entitled "Cannibal Carpenter."

> He wants to build you a house
> out of your own bones, but
> that's where you're living
>   anyway!
> The next time he calls
> you answer the telephone with the
> sound of your grandmother being
> born. It was a twenty-three-hour
> labor in 1884. He hangs
>   up.

Since Brautigan's grassroots popularity had circumvented the established literary publishing ladders, his work was held up to a withering critical crossfire from, in Tom McGuane's words, "the beans and franks reviewers." Subject to scorn and condescension among the literary establishment, parodies of his fiction were performed by Walker Percy in the *New York Times* and by Garrison Keillor in *The New Yorker*. When Brautigan experimented in the late 1970s with novel genres, writing what he called Gothic-Westerns and other mixed-breed fictions, these books and/or his persona were subject to such reviews as this:

> And so, as from the id's own pit, there arises the persona of the author of *Dreaming Of Babylon*—not Brautigan, nor yet C. Card, the novel's less-than-cardboard narrator, but the ineffably dopey, possibly meth-drinking cretin whose poverty-stricken imagination is the (imagined) source of this ramshackle mass of bad jokes, stupid ideas, and plain nonsense.

One day in the middle 1970s while we were in a bookstore, Richard showed me a tell-all book written by someone who used to work for the *New York Times Book Review*.

"I was killing some time one day, and I found this book so I turned to the index to see if I was mentioned." Richard said. "And I noticed I was on one page, so I turned to that page and I found out that they had a special hatchet man for reviewing Kurt Vonnegut and myself, no matter what we published."

Although by then Richard often pretended to be sophisticated about such matters, actually he was amazed and hurt that these attacks were routine procedure. His defense was that his work was a uniquely West Coast-style of writing, and said, "It doesn't get east of the Rockies."

But in the beginning of his fame, Brautigan didn't need critics. That alone was enough to doom his good writing to mediocre reviews. Fellow writers—such as Guy Davenport and Tom McGuane and Don Carpenter—were able to respond to and articulate the discipline, seriousness and skill with which

Richard wrote. In one of the few favorable reviews of Brautigan published in the *New York Times*, McGuane made these remarks.

> For what is important is that Brautigan's outlandish gift is based in traditional narrative virtues. His dialogue is supernaturally exact; his descriptive concision is the perfect carrier for his extraordinary comic perceptions. . . ."

Guy Davenport saw the major conflict of *Trout Fishing* as residing between the narrator's consciousness and the world.

> Mr. Brautigan's solicitude for the world he lives in and his impatient grasp of essences continue their clear emergence in [the] opening paragraph all the way through an inspired book. . . . [Brautigan is] a kind of Thoreau who cannot keep a straight face. . . . I would place him among the philosophers, for his central perception is that the world makes very little sense to a man with a plain mind.

Although such rave reviews turned out to be rare, Brautigan never bowed to anyone else's opinions. He could be quite candid about the qualities of his writing. Around 1970, when his poetry was being sold in editions of thousands and getting trashed in the few reviews written on it, he was puzzled and a bit incredulous at the virulence of these responses.

After showing me one such review, he remarked, "I'm a minor poet. I don't pretend to be anything else."

Of course, in reality he wanted to have things both ways. He always tried to return to his fiction for protection from these attacks, insisting that his novels were what mattered, but by then he was dependent upon public adulation and his work had become an emblem of something far larger than his skill as a writer.

When his public fame was at its height in the early 70s, Richard was generous with his contacts. He was conscientious about sharing his good fortune and happy to provide leads for his friends. However, he was aware that he was regarded as a fluke by the literary people on both coasts. While he was realistic about the strength of any influence he might wield, Richard was still very persistent about advancing work by writers he cared for, although he was seldom successful.

By 1974, after having provided some blurbs for friends' books which did not do well commercially, he joked that "a blurb from me is the kiss of death."

In my own case, no matter how Richard tried to help, providing me with various introductions, nothing seemed to work out particularly well. This also became one of our running private jokes, that he was "managing" my literary career—a euphemism for my visits to San Francisco and the parties we attended. This manager routine started in Monterey while I was living there in 1971. Richard was on a visit, staying with Price Dunn's brother, Bruce, during the Easter vacation.

To celebrate Richard's newest book of short stories, a party was planned. To bolster the attendance, I invited my friend John Veglia, a teacher at a private high school outside Monterey, to bring along some of his students. One of them, a good-looking blonde, was being visited by her boyfriend from back east, and he happened to be an editor of a literary journal at an Ivy League college. This editor wanted to meet Richard very badly, to solict some work for an issue of exciting new West Coast writing. When I told Richard about this chance, he said that my work ought to be in there too. And he vowed that he would arrange everything.

At the party Richard, the editor and I hit it off right away. We spent most of the time in a corner, yakking about literary gossip. When the editor asked Richard for some work, he said he would send some short stories but that the editor also had to take a look at chapters from my first novel, *Gush*. Impressed by Richard's enthusiasm, the editor agreed. With the white wine flowing freely, everything seemed set.

When the editor left for a trip to the john, Richard, pleased with his literary politicking, said, "There, you see how easy it is?"

While all this was going on, the editor's girlfriend had been ignored and she got upset. Price later said, with his own inimitable candor, that "she was out in the kitchen, swabbing down the tonsils of every man she met." She happened to run into Bruce who, overprepared for the party, was in a generous Irish euphoria. When she asked him to dance, he became the perfect host and said yes.

As the editor sat down beside us, about to resume our literary chat, he looked up and saw his girlfriend out on the dance floor with Bruce. Even though rock was blasting out of the stereo, Bruce and the woman were doing a very slow dance. This dance seemed to require that they hold each other close and french-kiss a lot.

The editor stood up, went over to them, and tapped Bruce on the shoulder. Bruce looked up from his dancing and the editor hit him in the face. It wasn't what Bruce was expecting. Just a moment earlier he had a nice hot tongue in his mouth and now he had a fist.

As this difference registered, a perplexed look crossed Bruce's face. When he stepped away from the woman, the editor hit him again.

Bruce was still thinking about these two events, as the editor circled to Bruce's right, expecting a return punch. Bruce followed him around, almost as if he were now slow-dancing with the editor, instead of his girlfriend. The editor kept his eye on Bruce's right hand, waiting to block a punch, and Bruce, who was left-handed, knocked him through the french door.

The flight through the door looked just like the movies— glass and frame disintegrating around the flying editor as he went skidding out onto the front porch. From our seats on the floor, Richard and I watched his girlfriend rush out to comfort the editor and take him away to her car.

After a moment of silence. Richard took a drink and then, with beads of white wine hanging from his moustache, stared at the fragments of the door.

"Keith, you know, things haven't been working out for you lately," he said. "I think what you need is a literary manager. How about me?"

Brautigan had strong sexual urges, but his love life seems to have been as complex and idiosyncratic as his other habits. Fame complicated matters. His friend Mary Anne Gilderbloom was amazed at how many women hit on Brautigan in public. One night in a cafe a woman threw herself at his feet. Mary Anne was impressed by how he rescued the embarrassing situation, humoring the woman back on her feet and treating her kindly. Brautigan started his relationship with Mary Anne in a courtly fashion by reading her poetry and taking her to long talky dinners. When members of her family suffered through some medical disasters, Brautigan continually inquired about them, offering help. "He almost seemed to adopt my family. He was always so courteous and concerned."

On the flip side, *Rolling Stone* reported that in North Beach his S&M practices were common knowledge. Yet when I talked to his friends and lovers, only one knew of a rumor. I assumed Richard had experienced it, since he wrote about bondage in his novel, *Willard and His Bowling Trophies*. An S&M pattern would be consistent with the abuse he suffered in his childhood and with Brautigan's need for control. But, given North Beach's insularity and our mutual friends, certainly more people I know would have gossiped about it, so I have reservations about how frequently these things happened. I suspect any incidents of this nature were confined to one-night stands.

While his cafe crawls remained a constant, his harem days of the 1967 summer did not last long. As Lani commented, "He had enough loneliness, he didn't need to add the burden of continual one-night stands." But he returned to that life when his partners left. Serial girlfriends were usually the rule, one at a time, but most relationships never lasted more than a few years. They were strained because, as his friend Valerie Estes said, "Richard was always on the make." He loved the North Beach night life where the sexual hunt is always present. Don Carpenter remarked that Richard was the last to leave a bar if there were any women around. Under those conditions Brautigan's romantic gallantry disappeared. Stories of him accompanying a casual pickup to her apartment and immediately taking off his clothes were hot gossip. In his salad days his endurance for the hunt seemed as capacious as his ability to drink. After the literary groupies descended on Brautigan, he tried to maintain a self-image as a stud, but it was not very convincing. One girlfriend commented they had spent their first week together almost entirely in bed. Another said that, after some time together, she severed the relationship because, among other reasons, "the sex wasn't what it was cracked up to be." Brautigan always needed companionship, but his nocturnal habits seldom led to a stable home life.

If there was one trait common to all his steady girlfriends, it was intelligence. "I find intelligence in a woman to be an aphrodisiac," he wrote. He enjoyed sharing intellectual pursuits with women, but normally only during the courtship days. Then he spoke at length of what his girlfriends were doing, but once the romance had cooled and the forging of emotional commitments started, talk of them stopped, even if they were still living together.

Since Richard's women friends tended to be smart, few had any intention of creating a life-long bond with Richard. Most sought different ways of looking at the world, something Brautigan provided quite easily. Women who took up with him weren't looking for a husband. They wanted spontaneity, and they certainly didn't lack it, even if with Richard this sometimes had its diabolical side. That was the trade-off.

"One of the more complex things about Richard was his mood changes," his girlfriend Siew-Hwa Beh commented. "There was no pattern. It could be hour to hour, it could be days. A lot of that was mediated by drinks, but it was very hard to deal with. He could go from being real exuberant to very dark and depressed, or he could get mean and nasty, or nostalgic or sentimental, and sometimes transcendent, philosophical. Richard wouldn't ever talk about what was upsetting him, though. Instead, he'd tell a story or think of something witty."

Brautigan's unpredictability extended into daily life in odd and endearing ways. Valerie Estes remembers Brautigan trying to repair a shower curtain in their apartment. He found the solution with some green Italian tape. The discovery so charmed him that he became a regular Mr. Fix-it. "After that, when I came home, I'd look forward to what new thing would be swathed in green Italian tape," Valerie said. "Pretty soon it seemed like everything in the house had green Italian tape somewhere on it."

Other of his enthusiasms were more infectious. His artist friend Marcia Clay related how he was fascinated with Japanese novelists but had no one with whom to discuss them. When he found out she hadn't read the writers, he took her to Japantown and bought a stack of novels. Since Marcia spent her nights painting, the perpetual night-owl Richard would drop by her studio and talk about Kawabata, Tanizaki and Kenzaburo Oe into the morning.

While he enjoyed being picked up because of his fame, he also liked it when his media-image was unknown. Siew-Hwa Beh initially attracted Richard because she didn't know his work. When she asked what he did, he told her he wrote *Trout Fishing In America*. She told him she didn't know anything about sports, that she studied films. Around her, Brautigan seemed freed of his hippie image. Movies were an addiction to him, anyway, and her inside knowledge fascinated him, along with the film crowd in which she moved.

Socially, Brautigan enjoyed the company of women. "I feel close to women. Often I can ask them questions it would be harder for me to ask a man. Women are more likely to humor my strange ideas." Women's opinions mattered to him, but mostly he catered to single women and ignored wives. Brautigan had the irritating macho habit of never referring to his men friends' partners in conversations. Lani dubbed herself and our mutual friends' wives "Brautigan widows," because Richard took their husbands along on his night crawls and seldom included the women. When I told Richard about this title, he was embarrassed and a little chagrined. As a peace offering, Richard invited Lani and Bruce Dunn's girlfriend Cindy to accompany him and his girlfriend on a tour of North Beach night life. Dinner and drinks and entertainment were all covered, as reparations for any previous domestic damages. After this gesture of appeasement, however, Lani spent the next day in bed, moaning about Grand Marnier milkshakes. Requests for an encore were never forthcoming.

The situations with his lovers inevitably turned rancorous. Even in relationships that were founded on Brautigan's respect for the woman's intellect, his paranoia about women's powers over his emotional life surfaced. This profile is common for victims of child abuse. He tested his lovers, pushed them away and demanded constant attention and affection. He deserted them for his North Beach bachelor habits, including the familiar double standard that most bohemian men seem to cherish. These habits also reinforced this pattern of abandoning his partners to the home. Sometimes, probably out of guilt for his own behavoir, he'd force the image of homemaker on women.

"Neither of us wanted children," Siew-Hwa related, "but he came home one evening—he was a bit drunk and sort of sad—saying, 'I know you'll want children; you're only twenty-eight, twenty-nine.' He was afraid of the responsibility."

"Richard destroyed the relationship—I'm not uncomfortable saying that. He started initiating a lot of destructive things that would cause rifts, like staying away until all hours of the night. He never brought women back to the apartment, but he would see another woman and come home and say, 'Oh, now there are three of us.' I'd say, 'Richard, you're causing the breakup, and if you cause it, you can stop it.' We were together for two years—it seemed like a decade, it was so intense."

Protection of his talent, the one thing that had saved him from a life of poverty, was paramount. He also genuinely could not find any way to change the character he'd been given by his upbringing. He discussed this with Siew-Hwa.

"He was fond of saying, 'Nobody changes. I don't believe in change.' That, I think, was the tragic flaw: he could have laser-beam insight, but somehow he was suspicious of analysis. Analysis would somehow take away his craft, his skill, his talent. He'd listen to you, and sometimes things seemed OK; then all of a sudden the darkness would come over him and he'd say, 'No, it's not possible.' "

Some women found it easier to be a friend to Richard than a lover, and a few of his girlfriends maintained relationships with him throughout his life. Valerie Estes was one, and he respected her academic accomplishments. When she won a Danforth scholarship for graduate school, he called me to announce the good news. She also was capable of deflating his inflated self-importance. During the 1970s, when he left a saccharine message on his answering machine tape about how he was out in a beautiful sunlit day, she skewered this nonsense with an acerbic reply, telling him to come off that out-dated flowerchild crap. He delighted in telling me about this, but by then they were just friends. Such criticism was not tolerated from his romantic partners and they found it too hard to remain close to a man who allowed himself to be distracted by any pretty fan.

I was always amused that Brautigan's fans thought of him as a functional human being, in an everyday masculine sense. He wasn't. He could be suspicious of the simplest household matters. Ianthe recalls when she was a teenager he warned her never to attempt to replace a light bulb by herself. He insisted that instant death and dismemberment might result. His welfare class background accounted for much of this. Brautigan once said, in reference to canned food, "I was taught that food could kill you." He told Ianthe a story of when the welfare department placed his mother and her family in a motor court with gas stoves. Terrified of explosions, his mother refused to light the stove; she prepared cold meals instead and stayed up night after night, sniffing the stove for leaks.

Brautigan's view of the physical world resembled a Buster Keaton comedy where inanimate objects conspire to strip the hero of his dignity and peace of mind. He never learned to drive. He only owned a car late in life when he lived on a ranch in Montana, and then it was for guests to ferry him into the nearby towns of Livingston or Bozeman.

When fans descended on him, sometimes their assumptions created wonderful comedy. After arranging to take some new fans by his Geary Street apartment, one of his favorite asides was, "Wait until they get a look at Chez Brautigan."

He was aware of his own eccentricities and he could be droll about his primitive aspects, as in his description of Richard Brautigan, a character in *The Abortion,* and author of the unpublished novel, *Moose:* "The author was tall and blond and had a long yellow moustache that gave him an anachronistic appearance. He looked as if he would be more at home in another era." Richard delighted in the contradiction, and it was this, along with his serio-comic terror of physical change, which kept him in his ratty Gothic ghetto apartment for so many years after he struck it rich.

"My friends keep telling me to move," he'd joke. "Maybe I better. I've noticed that when I bring a new girlfriend home, they sometimes have a change of attitude about our relationship when they see," and he'd pause, putting on a sombre Gothic tone, "The Museum." This allusion to the horror movie *The Wax Museum* was the name that the artist Bruce Conner had dubbed his apartment and its shelves of tatty junk and rusty mementoes.

When money and fame propelled him into a world of movie stars and Hollywood advances, Brautigan was not at home there, even though through the first five years of his wealth he succeeded in becoming cosmopolitan, traveling to Europe and New York. His recognition of the downhome reality of his life provided much of his humor. When he eventually gave up his funky lifestyle, he lost an important part of himself as a writer.

This funkiness also had its grim side. Brautigan's periodic existential bleakness, which was forged in his childhood, at times caused him to enjoy inflicting this view on unsuspecting others. His insistence that "we are all in the same sad mess" was a carryover from adolescence. Richard never lost this point of view. No amount of money or success could ever remove it from his psyche. Brautigan had been on the bottom of society. Some part of his private self always remained the outsider, no matter how much his public self was co-opted.

At times he trashed sentimental pleasures of others out of the rage and frustration he harbored toward society and his family history. He spent Christmas in porno theaters and would detail bleak meals in deserted restaurants on Thanksgiving. He pretended to be proud of not belonging, of having no real family.

In later years he loved to talk about how the Japanese got drunk, and how their behavior was forgiven the next day because the offended recognized that the offenders were drunk. This was a child's view of Japanese manners, but it offered him some solace while his own pride and alcoholism sent him further and further away from any society. Not knowing the language, he viewed Japan as if it were fictional, creating his own narrative and reading his own meanings into its patterns.

If pride sustained Richard through his lean years, once he was famous and his work parodied and ridiculed, his pride only allowed him to adopt angry amusement and his own skyrocketing sales as a defense. When the sales dropped, his angry amusement turned to plain anger, and thence to bitterness and fear, and finally to a kind of loathing which poisoned his spirit and partly eliminated his ability to respond to life and its small happinesses.

"When fame puts its feathery crowbar under your rock" was how Richard ruefully phrased it, and as usual he was being accurate about his own case when he said rock. Brautigan was like a strange creature released into the world, but this did not prevent people from liking him and actually feeling quite protective toward him.

My theory is that Richard perpetually looked like what some people felt like when they were going through adolescence. I think that this quality made people remember those days when their bodies were growing so rapidly that they felt as long and tall and awkward as Brautigan looked and acted. Richard never seemed quite in control of his body, and he certainly had only marginal control over his lively imagination.

At heart he was a showoff. If Richard had a god, it was Pan. He loved panic, spontaneous outbursts of emotion that cleansed the heart. Once, while talking over the phone, he got in an argument, tore the phone out of the wall and threw it into the fireplace. Unfortunately a fire was burning. When he recovered from his fit, and remembered how hard it had been to get a phone installed, the money it cost, he tried to rescue it, scorching his hand. It was a story that he loved to tell on himself—another aspect of his need to display his moods.

Some women were attracted to his penchant for acting out his emotions. These displays were more often quite tender and gentle, too, and he was extremely sensitive to other people's social liabilities and personal chagrins. Marcia Clay recalled this side of Brautigan.

> I was born with cerebral palsy, and Richard was very sympathetic to that. He saw this hand was cramped. I never wanted to call attention to it; I kept all my watches and rings on my right hand. One day he took both my hands very ceremoniously and said, 'This right hand is very beautiful; it doesn't need any jewelry. Put your jewelry on your other hand; it needs all the help it can get.'

When bored he was capable of anything. He told me about being held up at a friend's house, waiting for his return. Another friend dropped by, and they waited together, drinking to pass the time. After several hours, the friend hadn't returned, so Richard and his partner emptied the friend's refrigerator and painted the kitchen wall with mustard, mayonnaisse and jam.

When Brautigan was slighted or insulted, he rarely reacted immediately. He would swallow his anger. To anyone who knew him, this would become visible: his face flushed, his expression froze, and then, with great difficulty he'd compose himself and start plotting revenge. One incidence of this occurred at a lunch on Union Street.

When I arrived Richard was quite relaxed and amiable. A literary agent from the East Coast was at the table and we commenced chatting and drinking. Richard mentioned something about one of his early books.

The agent said, quite offhandedly, "Oh yes, I saw that," recalling that he had rejected the manuscript. It was clear from his tone that he still regarded the novel as an inferior piece of goods. It was the kind of passing cut that comes so naturally to those in the literary world.

Richard stiffened, and his face went beet red. To cover his anger, he took a drink of wine. The conversation continued and, after a few minutes, Richard casually remembered that this same book had just gone into its tenth printing. He acted very bemused. He claimed that he was just as surprised as everyone else at his good luck. Then, without looking at the agent, but just scanning the passersby, he listed, in a haphazard manner, all the other editions which his books had gone through—and at that time none were out of print. He did this quite easily, idly recalling those editions of nine or eleven or fifteen printings, the advances and royalties and foreign sales.

It was one of funniest and cruelest things I'd seen him do because the agent, no matter how hard he tried, obviously could not stop calculating the money he would have made, handling those books for ten percent. After sitting through Brautigan's recital, the agent soon found a reason to leave and excused himself.

It was the only time I ever heard Richard recount the financial side of his writing in such detail. When the agent was gone, Richard took a sip of his wine, looked at me with a slight smile and said, "There's an old Italian saying, 'Revenge is a dish best eaten cold.' "

Fame creates a certain diastole in a writer's life. At the opening phase new experiences rush in, and the task is to react to all these and find room for them. Brautigan was happy at the attention and pleased with his new social mobility. At first, he generously tried to share his good fortune and new friends with his old friends. This led to disasters, both social and physical.

Brautigan brought his friend actor Rip Torn down to Monterey for a trout fishing trip to Big Sur. Torn was driving a rental station wagon with a two-man kayak strapped to the top. He seemed high-strung and nervous, chainsmoking handrolled cigarettes.

At Price Dunn's house, Brautigan invited me and Price's

brother Bruce along on this expedition. I declined. Brautigan told Rip that Price knew every inch of Big Sur, but I knew that Price hadn't been in the Santa Lucia mountains for years. There could be only trouble ahead if he was going to be their guide. Besides, it was the dry season. I wondered where the hell they'd find any streams, let alone fish. There was also something a little haphazard about Mr. Torn's morning behavoir which didn't give me confidence in his driving skills, especially when I remembered Big Sur's back-country roads.

When they returned that evening, both fenders of the station wagon were chalky red and dented from the rubdowns that the canyon walls had administered. Bruce informed me that Rip had used the Big Sur massage service going in and coming out, as an aid to braking.

Most of the streams were about the size of a man's wrist. Crawling up canyons lined with poison oak hadn't been the fun they'd expected. And Richard was bitter about their catch. He'd caught a water snake.

To cover up his disappointment in Price's skills as a guide, Richard dubbed Price and Bruce "The Blunder Brothers." Since he'd returned the papier-mâché bird, Willard, to Price that visit, he made up a fantasy about their adventures capturing the dreaded water snakes of Big Sur. Littered around the living room were bowling trophies Price had been given in a hauling job. They were incorporated into the fantasy of the Blunder Brothers, but under the fantasy was a sour feeling, as if Price and Bruce hadn't come up to the mark.

Celebrity shrinks life, too and a predictable narrowing of experience results. Fame connects a writer with other famous figures and while stars are often very good material for fiction, their stories are already well-known. Not only that, daily enthusiasms may have been acquired from other celebrities. These fads, picked up by the press, eventually spread to the public. So if X is going to India to study with a master, by next year everyone else is, too. It is stale news. Discretion plays its part. When your friends are famous, their secrets can't be fictionalized as easily as when your friends are not public figures.

To avoid this lack of new material, some writers use their popularity to finance various explorations by writing journalism. Brautigan was no reporter and had no recourse to journalism. For what assignments came his way—such as an introduction to a paperback edition of Beatles songs—he spun out short, metaphorical fantasies. While his fiction often sprang from his imagination, he was no different than any other fiction writer: he depended on his friends for topics and fresh material.

However, by the end of 1975, I was optimistic that Richard seemed to have come to terms with this particular difficulty of fame. Owning a house in Bolinas and a ranch in Montana seemed to have grounded him, giving him things to do. The Western experiences in Montana had helped him finish his first novel in seven years, *The Hawkline Monster*. The critical and popular reception of this book indicated that he was reaching a wider audience than simply young people. And for the first time his work was optioned by Hollywood.

Most importantly, he had arrived at a more stable emotional life with a new woman friend, Siew-Hwa Beh. He became very domestic with her, cooking meals and living more quietly than in previous years. "A lot of people think of him as being sexist and male-chauvinist," she said, "and he was certainly capable of all that, but to me he was a perfect house-husband. He would cook every day, broil salmon, make his famous spaghetti sauce, or just fill avocado halves with shrimp. It was the first time he ever had a real home." Active in what she called "guerrilla" movie projects, Siew-Hwa had also edited an anthology of women's writing on films, and she interested Richard in such subjects as *film noir*.

When his friends engaged him in their pursuits, Richard was always happier, whether it was watching pro basketball or studying WWII tactics. The enthusiasms of his acquaintances drew him out of the shell of solitude so necessary for creating fiction.

Brautigan made a break from his hippie celebrity past in 1975 when he finally moved out of his Geary Street slum and into a newly remodeled apartment on Union Street. In his dank apartment the anachronism of Richard's hippie past was all too evident. Young and eager acolytes had passed through, leaving their gifts. A stuffed cloth trout, naive childish calendars, and a handmade quilt for his brass bed were still there, along with mimeo Digger dollars and "God's eyes." Some fan had given him a WWII Japanese machine gun. Richard said the machine gun reminded him of how he learned to read. Apparently at age six he understood a headline about the Japanese attack on Pearl Harbor and that was when he first made the connection between letters and reality. But it was time to leave and he asked me to help pack up the stuff for storage and truck his goods to the new apartment.

On the last day of moving, I brought along my seven-year old daughter Persephone. Children generally liked Richard, recognizing an ally in anarchy, but that day Persephone was grumpy. Richard, hung over, was quite solicitious. He promised her all kinds of ice cream goodies at Enrico's when we finished loading his stuff on my truck. She would have nothing to do with promises and sat glumly in the kitchen with a Coke that Richard had hurriedly brought from the Cable Car Drive-in around the corner.

The last boxes to go were stacked in the living room, and I carried them out, leaving it bare of everything but money. Richard had a habit of emptying his pockets of change on the floor each night. Around the front room, there were all kinds of coins. I'd heard earlier the story about how he had acquired the habit in the late 50s.

One spring, when he was totally broke in San Francisco, a friend had called and promised him a job in Reno as a laborer on a construction project. Richard borrowed enough money to get to Reno, but once there, he was told the job wouldn't start for three days. He had no money for a room and very little for food. On his first night he had a series of comic encounters with a Reno cop who kept finding him curled up on park benches. Threatened with jail, Richard hiked to the outskirts of town and found an old easy chair abandoned in the corner of someone's suburban yard. For three nights he waited until their lights went out and then he slept in the chair wearing three sets of clothing to ward off the cold night air.

"The last thing I put on was a quilted jacket and with all those other clothes on, I looked just like a Chinese communist," he said. "You can imagine what those Nevada folks would have done if they woke up early and found one of them in their backyard."

At the end of his first day on the job, Richard drew an advance. After he paid for his motel room, he was so happy to have any money at all, he yanked out his pockets and sprayed change all over the room, a practice he had continued ever since.

Anyway, on our last moving day, Richard was facing reality from inside one of his mental whirlwinds, hung over and sour with worry. More to distract him than my daughter, I suggested that he give her the job of sweeping the floor. At first Richard didn't understand what I was saying. He thought I was suggesting child labor or something. Then he recognized what was on his floor. He marched to the back porch, got the broom and dustpan, and brought them to Persephone, who was staring at the gas range in terminal boredom.

"Persephone," he said, holding them out to her, "would you like to sweep my floor?"

She looked up at me with the universal do-I-have-to question in her eyes. I nodded. She sighed and took the broom and dustpan from Richard.

"No, not the kitchen floor," Richard said, pointing. "The floor in there."

As she passed by me, Persephone gave me one of her sideways looks—*your weird friends*—and dragged the broom into the next room.

Richard was in an ecstasy of expectation as Persephone wearily dropped the dustpan on the book shelf and then looked down at the end of the broom. There was a wonderful moment as her eyes saw the money and then glazed over with childish greed. He could barely contain himself. In his glee he hopped to his back porch and came out with an empty mayonnaise jar and held it out to Persephone. She glanced up, jerked it out of his hand, put it on a shelf, and then the broom really began to fly, sweeping up piles of quarters, dimes, nickels and pennies. I like to think back to this day, the look on Richard's face as he stood in the doorway, his hangover banished, watching delightedly as Persephone swept his floor clean. He knew that this would become a legend of her childhood. Spare change was a good way to leave his Geary Street apartment and the 1960s.

V. Bolinas

hen Richard bought a Bolinas country house in the early 1970s, I thought it a wise move. There he entertained people who had helped him in previous years, something he couldn't do in his Geary Street dump. He needed a retreat from the temptations of San Francisco where his habitual afternoons at Enrico's provided him with a surplus of young women, all in love with his fame. He also needed a place to park himself after his writing jags—which left him exhausted, nervous and plagued with insomnia. But, as with most things Richard did, the house turned out to be a mixed blessing.

I heard about the Bolinas house from Price, who accompanied Brautigan on the first furniture moving jobs. I imagined it to be a sunny and bright oceanside place up on the Bolinas mesa. Instead, the house turned out to be a tall old redwood three-story with a big deck in front. With no view of the ocean, it was set back under some trees on a slope facing more trees. My first impression was the house was dark, damp and shadowy. I couldn't figure out why Richard had bought it. With his money he could afford a house facing the ocean with lots of light.

Later, in Monterey, I asked Price why Richard took that particular house. Price snorted at Richard's folly. "Ah, Keith, it reminds him of a Northwest tree-house, that's why he bought it. He can look out any window and only see trees." By 1973 I was living in Berkeley. Because I had a truck and no steady job, Richard enlisted me for his various attempts to make the house habitable. On my first day, I trucked in boxes of books and

such for storage downstairs. Richard was coming out later that
afternoon from San Francisco. While I was having a look
around, I wandered upstairs and found three bedrooms and a
bath. The last place I looked in was the east bedroom. Set in a
corner of the house, it was quite small and filled with junk, bed
frames and such. As I was leaving, I turned and had the strong
sensation that someone was there. In my mind's eye, almost
like a slide being placed in a projector, I saw a girl in a white
nightgown. I didn't think much of it, it was so fleeting. I
assumed it was just a mild hallucination.

That night when Richard arrived, I made a joke about it.
"Who's the girl in the corner bedroom?"

Richard blanched. "You s-s-saw her?" he stuttered.

"Sorta, I didn't really see, I only had this sensation," I said.
"Who is she?"

"I don't know," Richard said. "But you are the fourth person
who has seen her upstairs. You don't know the other three who
saw her, so I've got to believe you."

It seemed comically right to me that there should be a ghost
in the corner bedroom of Richard's new house. A short story in
Revenge of the Lawn told about his boyhood fearlessness in the
face of the supernatural. I thought a ghost was perfect com-
panion for his Northwest Gothic sensibilities to mull over.
Ianthe told me less benign stories about the ghost, how it
would walk up and down the stairs at nights and scare the hell
out of her. Richard didn't seem terribly bothered by the ghost.
He was more curious than spooked by her. Later he researched
the history of the house and discovered that a young girl had
died there at the turn of the century. She was buried in the
backyard.

Richard once offered the Bolinas house to his friend Don
Carpenter, after Don's apartment had been damaged in a fire. I
helped Don collect any usable stuff from his place in San
Francisco and drove him to Bolinas. I was busy unroping the
load, when Don went into the house. He came right back out
and told me to pack it up again. He refused to stay there,
maintaining that the joint was haunted. He ended up taking all
his gear to Mill Valley. There he stayed with his ex-wife, rather

than live in the Bolinas house—an act he felt demonstrated the severity of his reaction to the house's ghostly ambience.

As his finances first bloomed, Richard planned to set up a foundation to help struggling artists. When he mentioned this idea to the poet Joanne Kyger, she told him it was one sure way for him to make a lot of enemies. She reminded him that poets generally take badly to the news of other poets' windfalls. She reminded him, too, how poets act toward their patrons. She said he would only put himself in a no-win situation. Brautigan was a soft touch, and so such notions remained on a personal level, via loans to writer friends. According to Ianthe, his records showed that practically no money was ever repaid.

Richard was always pleased to have his favorite people visit him in Bolinas. When he liked someone he would often go to amazing extremes to please them. In a way his methods were much like his writing. He would worry and fret over the smallest details, in order to have something come out right. Often this gave him tunnel vision, and nothing turned out the way he wanted. One funny example that comes to mind is an evening in Bolinas when Richard had Joanne Kyger, Don Allen, Bobbie Louise Hawkins and her husband, Robert Creeley, over for dinner.

Everyone showed up on time, except Creeley. When he finally arrived, he looked about one drink away from closing the only eye he had left. Richard, quite familiar with his condition, solicitiously ushered Creeley to the couch in front of the fireplace. There was a big fire and everyone was gathered around, having a glass of wine before dinner.

Bob apologized for being late, but he allowed that he had real trouble getting out of Smiley's bar in Bolinas. Apparently some admirers had cornered him there. But it became clear that he was more enthralled by some of his current ideas than by drink. Once he got comfortable on the couch, he seemed to imagine that he was at a party after one of his lectures. He began talking to himself in a language almost completely made up of abstract words, formulations, reifications and such, making it extremely hard to follow his line of thought. No one paid much mind to his steady stream of academic buzz words.

When Creeley left the room for a moment, Don Allen leaned over and asked Bobbie Louise if Bob had been unhappy lately.

"Not any more than usual," Bobbie said curtly—not being too thrilled with her husband's performance.

Just before dinner was served, Richard made a big show of putting on a Grateful Dead record. He said that he had been saving the record as a surprise for Creeley. Intensely involved with his train of highly abstract thought, Bob only nodded his thanks and then returned to his imaginary lecture.

When the first cut started, Creeley brought his head up abruptly. "This is my favorite on that record," he announced.

Richard beamed happily. As Creeley listened to the song, Richard told the story about all the obstacles that he had encountered during the day in his attempt to find this particular record for Bob. Content that he had made Creeley happy, Richard went back into the kitchen to attend to dinner.

When the song was over, Creeley staggered up, went over to the stereo and, trying to play the cut again, raked the needle across the record, ruining it. "Oh-oh," he said. Then he went back to the couch and resumed his discussion with himself.

At the sound of the record being ruined, Richard came rushing out of the kitchen and stood there watching the whole oh-oh performance by Creeley. Going over to the stereo, he brought out a second new copy of the album from the stack. In his own funny precise way, Richard congratulated himself. "I'm ready for Bob this time," he boasted. Then he went on to relate how Creeley had wrecked that very album on a previous visit.

Creeley barely acknowledged any of this. But, after Richard left the room, the first song finished once more and Creeley looked up and said, "That's my favorite cut." He went over to the stereo, lifted up the arm and then, skrreeak, ruined the second new album. "Oh-oh," Bob said, genuinely puzzled that this album seemed to be defective too.

Hearing the skrreeak of the needle being gouged across the record, Richard came back out of the kitchen. This time he had a very somber look on his face. Taking the record off the stereo, he carefully put it on top of the other ruined one. Then, with a look of rueful chagrin which was so common when his plans went awry, he trudged back to the kitchen.

Brautigan loved stories of artists' unbridled and eccentric habits in producing their art; they made him feel less freakish, I suppose, and more a part of a tradition. He romanticized the poet's life too, one mark of his roots in the North Beach hype with its self-destructive attitudes toward the art and the role of the artist. I never particularly cared for this, but I understood its place in Richard's life, given his apprenticeship in his youth to the poet Jack Spicer, who drank himself to death.

Of course, Richard was aware of the humor in such antics. The next morning I was out on the deck and I saw him walking around inside the house, picking up things. I assumed he was cleaning after the party. When Richard came outside, both hands were cupped in front of his face.

"Keith," he said, "do you want to see something?" He held out his hands. Scattered over his palms were many tiny pieces of paper, envelope flaps, and torn newspaper margins, each with indecipherable ant-like scrawls on them. "These are the latest poems of Robert Creeley. Whenever Bob comes over, he always leaves these lying around the house," Richard said. Then, with mock solemnity, he fixed his gaze on me and said, "I keep his collected new poems in a bowl above the piano for posterity."

Perhaps because of the tree house aspect of the Bolinas place and partly because of his pleasure in Creeley's company, Richard felt comfortable enough to open up about his childhood, a subject he had previously kept mysterious for good emotional reasons. One night, when we were with Creeley, I told some stories of my teenage gang in the Northwest; how once we stole from a driving range a gunny sack full of golf balls. Then we tried to figure what to do with them and ended up spending a Sunday morning driving them down a stretch of uncompleted freeway. It wasn't a driving contest; we did it just because the white balls showed up so well on the tan bulldozed dirt.

Richard talked about how his teenage gang was the same way, ready to do things simply because there was danger.

Once he related that he and his friends had been walking along and they'd come across a large dog—a Great Dane, if I remember right. Without a word, they picked up the Great Dane and carried it around. Richard made the point that his gang didn't know why they needed a Great Dane, but they were sure they'd find a use for one—it was an aesthetic decision, of sorts. Finally they came to a hospital. One guy went in to scout out the place, and then they carried the Great Dane into an empty operating room and left it there.

With considerably less humor he also remembered spending a night under a chicken house when the neighbors, having had enough of his gang's little tricks, went on a vigilante rampage. I believe this particular trick involved a balloon filled with chicken blood and water. Richard said that his gang took this uprising as a sign they should move their action out of their own neighborhood.

But most interesting of all were Richard's comments on his father. He claimed that he had only seen his father twice. The first time was in a hotel where, "I was pushed into this room and a man there gave me a silver dollar to go see a movie." The second time he saw his father he was in a barbershop. "He had shaving cream all over his face and I said who I was and he gave me some money to go see a movie that time, too."

When he told these stories, a particular look came over his face that he adopted whenever he was stonewalling something. A determined monotone crept into his voice then, and he would relate these things in plain, emotionally neutral sentences, as if saying, that's the way it is; that's all there is to this; these are the bare facts. He never would admit to being hurt; he would use this tone and attitude instead.

There was too much pain to stonewall. After Brautigan's death, Ianthe related how he had witnessed and experienced brutal abuse, abandonment, and neglect. One evening one of his stepfathers did not like the way his mother was cooking dinner. He picked up a skillet, knocked her out, and then continued making dinner using the same pan. One stepfather would rent a house, move them in and then skip town, leaving his family to be evicted. Broke, the family would go on public aid, moving into welfare hotels, and the stepfather would come back.

The cycle was inflicted on the children, too. Between the ages of six and nine Brautigan was abandoned three times. One afternoon he returned from school and found his mother and sister were gone with all their goods. He stayed in the empty house for week. Some neighbors tracked down his mother, collected bus fare, and sent him back.

Abuse was common and sometimes extreme. One of his stepfathers "would just thrash him and thrash him" and once tried to break his arm for some sin. He remembered being "rented out" with his sister for household chores. On one such occasion he was forced to watch his sister being whipped by a sadistic neighbor for some error.

He claimed his mother was the type of woman who loved children as babies, but ignored and feared them as they got older. When Brautigan had appendicitis, he was put to bed with a fever and left there. After five days, a neighbor alerted a local doctor. Richard recalled the doctor driving to the hospital at ten miles an hour, holding Richard in his lap for fear the swollen appendix would burst. The memory remained of the doctor's tears falling on him, as he wept out of rage and pity for Richard's condition. In typical fashion, Brautigan also remembered how funny the boy in the adjoining bed was, and how hard he had to work at not laughing, because of the pain of his stitches.

Apparently the cycle of abuse from stepfathers ended at age twelve, when his mother married a man who gave him some companionship, taking him hunting and fishing, beginning his lifelong love of those sports.

I never heard Richard allow his remembrances to get this graphic. Whenever he wrote of his childhood, he told stories of stark poverty and emotional desolation. In one of my favorite tales of his, "A Short History of Oregon," he ends with a vision of himself standing before an isolated house in the woods with rain pouring down. A bunch of ragged children stare at him from the porch. The yard is full of metal debris. He says, "I had no reason to believe that there was anything more to life than this."

At the time I imagined that by writing these short stories about his youth, Richard faced his childhood traumas and put them to rest. I believed, then, in the healing and redemptive qualities of art. I'm not sure that Richard ever agreed.

VI. Montana, 1976

"Too many things were out of proportion in his
life in relationship to their real meaning."
—*Sombrero Fallout*, 1976

W hen Brautigan invited me to his new ranch in
Montana in 1976, I had seen little of him in
previous months. He had been staying there and
that spring had gone to Japan for the first time.
The acceptance of his work in Japan had culmi-
nated in his forthcoming novel *Sombrero Fallout* being published
simultaneously in the United States and Japan. Richard was
quite proud of the welcome his writing had received.

Before he left for Tokyo, he showed me a Japanese edition of
his short stories and told me that this was now being used as
a textbook for teaching English.

"Not bad, huh pal, for a guy who took a couple of years to
get through first grade?"

He found it delightfully ironic that his work should be taught
in Japan when he had first learned to read from the 1941
headline, JAPS BOMB PEARL HARBOR.

Since Richard had been in Toyko most of the spring, he had
not been able to return to Montana in time to arrange for any
ranch work. He called me long distance and asked if I could
come up and help get the place in shape.

I told him I had not done any ranch work since I was
nineteen. He was so desperate that he offered to pay my way,
plus wages to compensate me for cancelling a job I had lined
up in Berkeley. I considered it a paid vacation and caught a
flight, planning to stay a month at the most, and then loop
around to Washington state to visit relatives.

I arrived on the Fourth of July, in time for the Livingston

105

Rodeo. Since Richard didn't drive, there was only a rental Dodge waiting for me at the airport. I was surprised to find that the actor Peter Fonda had rented the car on his charge card.

When I asked Richard why he had no plastic, he claimed that credit card companies routinely denied writers cards because of bad credit histories and bad characters. The way Richard told it, the denial was like a badge he had been awarded for being judged dangerous to banking.

This version didn't add up, because Richard now owned two houses, had sold books to the movies, and had lots of money in the bank. I chalked it off to one of his grandiose romantic fantasies about the social outrageousness of writers, but its whiff of megalomania set the tone for the events that soon followed.

Richard was busy with something, so I attended the rodeo with Peter and Becky Fonda. After the show, Richard and I hooked up for a tour of the Livingston bars, and later, when the bars closed, a Montana-style party with a bonfire of telephone poles. During this crawl I was drunk, sober, drunk and finally very tired and very sober again. Richard was difficult, if not impossible to detach from a party, and it wasn't until the last die-hards left that we got in the rental car for the ride home.

As we drove down the highway beside the Yellowstone River, Richard suddenly said, "Put it up to a hundred."

I couldn't believe I heard him say this. Richard was drunk, but in the past, even drunk, he had always shown an almost pathological fear of car wrecks. When I drove him across the Golden Gate Bridge on our trips to Bolinas, he always asked me to drive in the outside lane, away from the oncoming cars, since there were no traffic dividers on the bridge. He said he was terrified of head-on collisions. On the trip around Mount Tamalpais and along the twisting coastal highway, he also requested that I stay under thirty.

Since there was no traffic on the highway, to humor him I stepped on the gas, but slowed when I hit seventy.

"Faster," Richard commanded.

I punched it up to eighty.

"No. I want to go a hundred. Everybody goes a hundred here

in Montana, everybody does it," he insisted. "Put it up to a hundred."

So I floored it and eventually the Dodge, which was not a car I would have chosen for anything but trips to the Safeway, finally topped out at a hundred.

Richard was satisfied with that, and I slowed down immediately. He told me what a renegade state Montana was, how the Highway Patrol didn't enforce the fifty-five-mile-an-hour limit, and how true Cowboy Freedom was still possible there. At the time I thought it was just whiskey talking, and let it ride. But this phrase was used over and over during my stay. "In Montana everybody...."

I felt that in Montana Richard had granted himself license to override some of his strongest taboos. Either he'd become caught up in some fantasies, or he had convinced himself that he belonged and was doing what "everybody" did in Montana. Either way, for Richard, the perpetual awkward outsider, this was a dangerous notion.

On the afternoon of my second day there, July 5th, I had an even more unsettling glimpse of Richard's current state of mind. After breakfast, Richard said he had something to show me and he went into a cabin off the main ranch house. When he came back into the kitchen, Richard put on the table a .22 rifle, a beautiful old Remington pump action with a beveled barrel. "Isn't this a beauty?" he said.

As I picked up the rifle and admired it, Richard mentioned he'd never had it sighted in.

"I'll do it," I said. "There's time before we drive into Livingston this afternoon, isn't there? Where's a good place to shoot?"

Richard pointed out the kitchen window, indicating the old creek bank behind his barn. He said the ranch garbage dump was out there, and I could shoot at old tin cans against the bank.

"This really sends me back to childhood," I told him. "I spent years shooting tin cans in a quarry."

Richard smiled; he had a way of acknowledging such

emotions so gracefully—it was one of the pleasures of being around him. "Oh yeah, so did I. A .22 rifle, a box full of shells, and an old sandbank—that used to be heaven to me."

When I asked him if he wanted to come along, suddenly the smile was gone.

Richard turned away from me. "No," he said. "I don't like to go shooting with anyone else. I had an accident when I was young. Maybe you can take my daughter out. No one has shown her how to handle a rifle. She should learn."

"Oh sure," I said. I was a little nonplussed by the quick change of mood. I added that if Ianthe came back, I'd be happy to instruct her.

Richard got a box of ammunition from the cabin and put it on the table. I picked it up and walked out the back door and across the high grass of the lawn and continued up the path past the barn. In the ranch house I could see Richard watching me from the kitchen windows with a strange look on his face.

I realized I had forgotten to ask him where he was going to be. I thought I should have told him to call for me rather than come and get me. I didn't want any accidents.

As I set up the tin cans behind the barn, I thought that whatever his mood was, it was new to me. I wondered if it was because I'd never seen Richard around guns before.

After a while I stopped shooting. I thought about my own fears about someone coming around the barn and straying into the line of fire. Then I realized it wasn't me, it was Richard; I had gotten some contact paranoia off him.

Then I reran the look on his face as he stood on the porch. It was the pleased, guilty look of a boy about to risk something vicariously, by sending a pal out to do something he wouldn't do himself. Then I explored that look a little further, and decided it was as if he were expecting me to have an accident.

That realization really spooked me. I took the rifle back to the house, cleaned it, and put it in the corner of the kitchen where he could see it when he came back in.

Much later, as I mulled over the incident, I realized what had bothered me: Richard had never directly handed me either the rifle or the ammunition, almost as if absolving himself of any blame.

I never shot the rifle again, and Richard never mentioned it again. But when he took it out to his cabin that evening, he picked it up and glanced back at me with that same look—guilty complicity—and it made me extremely irritated. It was like seeing something unhealthy in my friend, something so creepy and adolescent that I never should have seen it.

The ranch buildings consisted of a large two-story house, a barn, and a shed which Richard had converted into his bedroom cabin. He had also built a writing room high in the loft of his barn, facing east and the Gallatin National Forest. With its isolation from the house and phone, with its breathtaking view of the mountains, the writing room seemed perfect. But I noticed that it also was bare, with few books or papers, only a typewriter and office supplies. I assumed this was because Richard had finished work on his latest novel. Two years after his death, Ianthe mentioned that the writing room had turned out to be nearly useless because of the millions of flies camped in the barn. It was only for show, and Richard did most of his work in his cabin.

Once I got a look around the grounds, it was clear that Richard was not exaggerating about the ranch. The property was in bad shape. Although he owned no livestock, he rented out the pastures. The fences needed mending and the fields needed cutting. The irrigation ditches also had to be dug out, so he could exercise his water rights. If he didn't water after a certain number of years, the rights were up for grabs by neighbors.

Except for keeping the water rights, Richard had no idea what needed doing. He relied on what his local friends told him about upkeep. Ironically, none of them were old ranchhands either, so Richard was not only a greenhorn, he was without much advice.

In addition to his helplessness at ranching, Richard had the extra handicap of being a non-driver living far out in the country. To get around he depended upon neighbors or the

Livingston taxis. So instead of a peaceful house away from it all, he had put himself at the mercy of others.

Once I set to work, I realized almost immediately that my real problem was not my rusty ranching skills, it was Richard: he was going through a serious crisis. Chronic insomnia was but one symptom, compounded by paranoia and too much drink.

For my own peace of mind, I set up a work routine. In the morning I got up around 5 A.M., made breakfast, and then went to mend fences before it got too hot. Late July afternoon temperatures were brutal in Montana, so I used that time for siestas. The first few days, Richard came rocketing into the kitchen in the morning, compulsively talking up a storm. He looked haggard and distracted and made little sense. He'd clearly not slept.

In the afternoons, when I wanted to nap, he wanted to drink wine and talk. The talks quickly became one-sided, consisting mainly of Richard's Byzantine grievances about running the ranch.

For the ranch house's remodeling, he had hired some people from Seattle, apparently old friends from the Haight-Ashbury days. He claimed that they had done a bad job. His stories of their ineptitude were later contradicted by other accounts I heard during my stay.

He was wary of hiring local people; he claimed he wanted to preserve his privacy. But at the same time he seemed unable to resist catering to the local appetite for gossip by his bad-boy behavior, reveling in the attention.

When the Seattle carpenters left—and according to a local legend I heard much later, it was at gunpoint—they abandoned their Nash Rambler. Richard was so enraged by what he considered their betrayal, he had Ianthe drive the Rambler around in circles in the pasture beside the barn until it ran out of gas.

Brautigan left the car there, but then told all his friends what he had done, and thereby added another twist to his neighborhood notoriety.

But this was nothing to "The Shootout at the OK Kitchen."

Locals were still talking about that when I arrived, though it happened the year before. This incident caused the most gossip and insured Richard's reputation for unbridled eccentricity.

After the spooky .22 incident on my second day there, I had come to conclusion that Richard had a very unhealthy attitude toward guns. In San Francisco, of course, I'd never seen him around guns, so this was also new to me. Raised on a Washington stump ranch, I'd been taught that guns were tools, dangerous ones, but still tools. To Brautigan they were instruments of revenge and caprice. Still, I also believed him when he claimed that he never went shooting with anyone else.

This was contradicted when Richard pointed out the picture frame above the refrigerator in the kitchen. Inside the frame was the face of a clock hanging from a nail, and in back of that was a bullet-marked wall. The rest of the wall around the frame had been replastered.

Richard told me proudly how one night the previous year he and Price had gotten a little drunk and shot out the kitchen wall. It started as a game, to see how close they could come to the number nine on the clock. "We were doing fine," Richard said, pointing at the bathroom off the kitchen, "until I climbed into the bathtub and tried a shot from there. That shot took out the clock."

When a local carpenter drove out to repair the damage, Richard took him to inspect the porch side of the wall first. The exiting .22 bullets had ravaged the wall and some deflected up through the roof, splitting the shingles. From the outside it wasn't clear how this damage happened, the wood only looked splintered. But when the carpenter got inside, it was obvious from the bullet holes in the kitchen wall how the damage had been done.

Until then Richard had said nothing. When the carpenter finished inspecting the four hundred-plus bullet holes in the kitchen wall, Richard shrugged and said, "I had some friends over last night, and . . . they got a little frisky."

As funny as this punchline was, upon reflection I got another dose of that same eerie feeling about Richard and guns. Richard told me this kitchen target practice story after the earlier incident with the .22, so it didn't add up. He would not go plinking but he and a buddy would shoot up his own house? I was used to contradictions in Richard's behavoir but this bordered on schizophrenia

Later, when I was back in California, I talked to Price about "The Shootout at the OK Kitchen." He said the idea was entirely Richard's.

"But that was nothing, Keith," Price told me, "The way it started was he wanted to go outside, at twelve o'clock midnight, and start shooting off those guns." Price had tried to dissuade him from the whole routine. "I told him, 'Richard, it's dark out there.' So, then he started blasting away at the wall. I figured that was better than doing it at night outside."

Besides showing Richard's love/hate relationship with the ranch, Price claimed that this was another instance of the macho behavoir which Richard felt his Montana friends required of him.

I didn't realize how much these two gun stories spooked me until later that week. I was at Peter Fonda's house, borrowing some tools. While I was talking to him, I walked around the front room, ostensibly admiring the Old West guns in his collection—but actually I was checking to make sure that they were all unloaded.

Peter noticed what I was doing. He was a little offended. He told me not to worry, that of course the guns weren't loaded. I'd grown up in a house with firearms, so I knew that guns were never kept loaded in the house. I apologized for my bad manners. I told him that once I had a near-fatal accident with a .22 pistol when I was young because of someone else's carelessness—which was true. I had been extra careful around guns ever since then. But Richard's attitude was the real reason why I became so nervous.

As my work on the ranch progressed, I saw that the upkeep was only one of the things disturbing Richard's peace of mind. He was a city person, used to the distractions and delights of urban life. In the country he had too much time on his hands and boredom set in fast.

On one hand, "The Shootout at the OK Kitchen" I could partially cross off to the same boredom that had once prompted Richard to paint a friend's wall in San Francisco with the contents of his refrigerator. But using guns in this way meant something more than just boredom. It implied loss of control, and that Richard had joined the people who imagine picking up a gun is supposed to remedy this.

Richard's ineptitude at scheduling his daily life was familiar to me, but now all sense of proportion seemed lost, both about his writing career and his social life. It frightened me. I had seen him loopy before, but not all the time.

There were very few instances when he regained his old detachment and his sense of humor. Except for some grim, rather macho kidding—of which the term "pal" was a new affectation for him—he seemed harried, manic and humorless.

Instead of the little vignettes of daily life that he habitually recounted (and later would turn into writing), there were stories of hobnobbing with Hollywood stars. His store of anecdotes began to resemble *People* magazine filler—how Warren Oates put down X or the time Richard beat Jack Nicholson one-on-one in basketball for fifty dollars, neglecting to mention that Nicholson was perhaps half a foot shorter.

These little fillers had powertripping as their subject. One of Richard's favorite ancedotes was an apparently true story he later included in his book, *The Tokyo-Montana Express.* "The Good Work of Chickens" is about a man who gets fed up with city people abandoning their pets out in the wilds. He follows one car home and later, as a comment on their cruelty, dumps a truckload of chickenshit on their front step. But the way Richard told it, revenge was the point, not the outlandishness of the reaction. In his earlier fiction, appropriately enough the short story, "Revenge of the Lawn," humor had been the effect of a vendetta.

My first big job was cutting the long summer grass around the house with a field mower I rented in Bozeman. After I finished the job, Richard came out and noticed that the cut grass revealed a soggy corner in the lawn. The dampness seemed to run under the northeast corner of the house. To my amazement he went into a tirade about the phone company. No one in America knew how to do anything. In America there was nothing but bad help anymore, unlike Japan.

At first I couldn't figure out what he was talking about, but then the story came out. Richard claimed that when the phone company laid the new cable for the valley, the irrigation ditch on the other side of the road had been damaged. This rupture allowed water to flow under the road onto Richard's property.

Richard's tirades went on all day; each time I came into the house, he was making another phone call, talking to phone company supervisors and claiming that they were the cause of his foundation problems.

The vendetta went on for two days, with Richard becoming more and more enraged, until the phone company refused to return his calls.

Then he called his lawyer in San Francisco. He was referred to a local lawyer, who affirmed that he had a right to protect his property in any way he wanted. Richard fretted for another day about hiring a backhoe to dig out the ditch on the other side of the road. His indecision alternated with tantrums against the phone company. I got very tired of hearing about it, so I took a look for myself.

Brautigan's house was situated on a low slope in front of the road passing north over Pine Creek bridge. Across the road to the east was a pasture that served as a drain field for Pine Creek. I walked up the grade, across the road and hiked to the corner of the pasture. From that vantage point I could see down the pasture and across the grade to Richard's house. The northeast side was clearly in the path of the original drainage for Pine Creek.

I tried to convince Richard of the futility of hiring a backhoe by explaining that some water would always follow the natural drain field, no matter how deep or thoroughly the ditch was dug. To prove this, I asked Richard to retrace my steps across the road to the far corner of the pasture.

"Imagine that the road and the grade aren't there, Richard,"

I explained. "Look at how the land lies. Imagine the water is coming from behind us. Gravity makes it run under the ditch, under any protective lining on the ditch, under the grade and directly past the corner of your house down to the creek."

"You got it wrong, pal." Richard said. "The phone company is responsible. My lawyer told me I am within my rights to dig out that ditch and remove any weeds that are causing this."

"But weeds aren't causing this. Gravity is. Gravity doesn't care about your rights. The water is simply following the lay of the land."

Richard remained unswayed. "No, it's the phone company's fault." He smiled grimly. "My lawyer will handle any problems."

He hired a backhoe operator, and the next morning the backhoe dug up the ditch. It also dug up the phone company cable and knocked out phone service for rest of the valley south of Richard's place. This didn't endear Brautigan to his neighbors.

The phone company sent a man to fix the cable. Richard, who became quite paranoid, sent me out to talk to him. The repairman said backhoes were always screwing up cables around there, no big deal. But Richard refused to believe my version or to talk to the repairman himself. He was sure a lawsuit was forthcoming. That night in his unrelenting turmoil about it, he called his San Francisco lawyer at 4 A.M.

"I forgot what time it was," he said, excusing himself from any blame. "My lawyer told me, 'Richard, don't ever call me this early in the morning, unless you've got a smoking gun in your hand and a body at your feet'."

Richard loved this comment and for the next few days he called up friends and told them the story.

These phone calls kept Richard out of my way, and I was happy working around the ranch. His behavior seemed excusable for a number of reasons. He had just finished proofing *Sombrero Fallout*, and, being such a perfectionist, he was usually a basket case after reading proofs. He had also just broken up with a girlfriend and still engaged in long-distance shouting matches with her over the phone. Jet-lag from his return to America and insomnia contributed to his drinking heavily. But none of these considerations really explained away the central feeling that I was getting.

Since the incident with the .22, it seemed to me something new and unhealthy was emerging in Richard's life: a bitter disrespect for other people, unless they had power. He regarded the foibles and minor vices that others displayed in their dealings with him as massive, intentional insults.

Since he was incapable of planning anything as complex as enough food for two days straight, let alone anticipate his other needs, he kept calling me in from the fields to make trips into Livingston. Sometimes this happened three times a day, until I told him that I couldn't do both jobs—ranch hand and driver. So he hired a housekeeper, a friend of the Fondas, who was staying in Livingston. At night his behavior became so erratic that the housekeeper and I arranged to take turns staying up with him. We tried to talk him down from his paranoid rants.

His rages about his career were even more disturbing. From his comments earlier that spring about his reception in Tokyo, I thought he was content with a second popularity in Japan, signaling that he had resigned himself to his waning popularity in America. But these rages were sometimes touched off by what I considered to be mild and rather innocuous events.

One afternoon, starved for reading material because there weren't many books at the ranch, I rummaged around in a cabinet and found a galley proof of a Raymund Mungo collection. I was reading on the front room couch when Richard entered. He prowled around the room a bit and then noticed what I was reading.

"You know what he said about a book of mine?" he asked me. He proceeded to quote a mildly negative comment by Mungo.

Then Richard paced around the room, bitching about its unfairness to him. He remembered something nice Mungo had said about his earlier work, but that only served as further proof of his perfidy. According to Richard, there was a conspiracy on to batter his later work with his more popular early novels. He ranted that no one in New York would touch those early works, or review them favorably when they were eventually published. After working himself into a rage, he marched from the room.

I was amazed by this tantrum. I was mulling it over when suddenly the back door banged open and Richard marched into the front room.

"Give me that book."

I handed it to him.

He ripped the proof copy apart sideways, then shredded the pages and threw everything out the front door onto the lawn. This Charles Atlas display of strength over, he went to his writing room in the barn. After about ten minutes he returned, holding another, inscribed copy of the same book. He read the inscription, laughed and tore up that book, throwing it out on the lawn with its destroyed proofs. Then he got some kerosene from the back porch and finished the job with a bonfire.

That night he appeared to have completely forgotten his little *auto-da-fé*. He spent most of the evening talking about his current censorship problems in a Northern California school district. He repeated every detail of the case over and over, quotes from principals and school boards and prosecutors. "The next sign to look for is book burning," he warned me solemnly, "just like the Nazis."

Later that night he calmed down and confessed he couldn't get to sleep anymore because he was afraid of his dreams. Whenever he just dropped off, his dreams would start and he couldn't stand the nightmares. I've never heard a writer confess anything more disheartening. I was very moved by his obvious suffering.

Richard said he had a prescription for Stelazine, which knocked him out for two or three dreamless hours. This second admission really shook me. I had never known him to take any drugs besides caffeine and alcohol. At the time his alcohol intake was from one to three liters of wine at dinner, and he often ended the night with whiskey. I told him to stop mixing the drug with alcohol because he'd kill himself. I also warned him that I didn't think Stelazine was commonly used as a sleeping pill; it was a long-term anxiety medication with a long list of side effects.

He did not want to hear that, so he didn't and went on to another subject. He wasn't taking much advice from anyone, including writers Tom McGuane and William Hjortsberg, two of his closest friends in Montana, whom he had called repeatedly during the drainage ditch fiasco without heeding anything they said.

I decided to limit the alcohol bought on our shopping trips, cutting the wine in half by buying fifths rather than the 1.5 liters of Alamaden that Richard liked, and I "forgot" to pick up brandy or whiskey. Most of the time he wouldn't drink alone, so I took car trips up in the canyons during the afternoon, thereby aborting any early starts on an evening's drinking. Less booze, combined with a fly fishing trip, calmed him down for awhile.

These maneuvers weren't just for Richard, they were also for me. His instability was frazzling. I had been with Brautigan on some pretty crazy nights and days in California, but I didn't think it went on all the time. It may seem naive, but I had assumed that when I quit, so did he.

Many of his friends flattered themselves that way, believing when they left Richard, the partytime stopped. But apparently, as his alcoholism progressed, the party raged on in their absences.

I wouldn't have lasted much longer, but some visitors arrived: an older Texan with two teenage sons. All three had spent several years in Montana and were on a nostalgic summer tour of local trout streams. The Texan was also trying to write a novel and asked Richard's advice. They obviously hero-worshipped Brautigan's fiction and also told good fishing stories. Under their influence, Richard suddenly blossomed into his old self, and his black moods vanished.

Around young people Brautigan was always at his best. He told jokes, asked questions and made them seem important and part of the gang. He also plied their father with questions about where the best fishing holes were, something the Texan knew well, and listened to his entertaining and hilarious stories of Livingston life. The Texan was an outsider, though he had lived there many years. He claimed it took two generations of winters before the locals accepted you. He had a wry and skeptical outlook on the habits of Montana folks.

While those three were there, providing Richard with distractions and companionship, life became a real pleasure, almost like the old days. When he got untracked from his problems, his humor was infectious, and it wasn't hard to forget about the recent past.

On the day they left, the Texan slipped out before breakfast, went to a secret fishing hole nearby and caught a huge brook trout. He presented it to Richard along with the gift of precise directions to this hidden "wagonwheel hole."

Only fishing for sport himself, Richard usually released any trout he caught, and hardly ever kept them for eating. If he did, he made sure they were young and pan size, ten inches long at most.

While he was thrilled with both presents and touched that the Texan had revealed where this fabled secret "wagonwheel hole" was, Richard was perplexed about what to do with a trout that size.

Holding up this monster, Richard walked around the house, muttering, "We can't eat all this. What the hell are we going to do with it? This is the Godfather of brookies."

The problem of its final disposition got Richard's imagination wound up, and the positive, obsessive flip side of his paranoia flowered. He embarked on a long, complicated and vintage Brautigan fantasy of nailing "the Corleone trout" up on a fence post under an old fedora beside the highway, "as a warning to those Brooklyn tourists cruising down from Yellowstone Park that they could be sleeping with the fishes tonight if they're not careful."

Eventually Richard put the Godfather trout in the freezer, but the situation diverted him for the rest of the day. Finally he decided to give it to Marian Hjortsberg, one of his favorite people, for a big dinner she was having soon. She baked it with spinach and he was delighted that it was used.

From Price Dunn and Richard's friend, Siew-Hwa, I had heard tales of the bad boy competitiveness that permeated the Montana scene. Siew-Hwa's versions of these macho displays were echoed by Price's account of the ranch. While Price held strong masculine attitudes, he was southern and he found these shows of rude manners and bullying offensive. While I was there, Richard's fantasies about belonging to a macho fraternity were clear, but none of the other men seemed to be involved.

What I saw were various artists busy with their families and businesses, all in sharp contrast to Richard's isolation, boredom and frustrations. I had a hard time seeing what he had in common with these people, other than fame. Richard professed great admiration for the writing of Tom McGuane and Jim Harrison. When I read their fiction, I saw little literary connection, except that their heroes were loners. Unlike Richard's protagonists, however, their heroes were rugged, competent men given to macho competitions.

I found nothing approaching the looney-tune life at Brautigan's ranch, except for a stint at Tom McGuane's house waiting for him to return with his power wagon so I could borrow it. During the two hours I was there, Tom's charming wife, the actress Margot Kidder, discussed her plans for bringing feminist philosophy to the ranchwives of Montana— a notion conceived, it seemed, independent of any local requests for the training.

The Montana people also seemed to have their senses of humor firmly in place. During one afternoon barbeque at McGuane's ranch, Brautigan spent half an hour detailing the tedious little improvements he had been making around his spread. None of this was at all interesting to his audience. Most drifted away except for McGuane's foreman, an old ranch hand named Millard Lambert.

He patiently listened to the spiel. When he judged that Richard had exhausted his store of picayune plumbing, roofing and remodeling minutiae, Millard nodded, then said, in a quiet voice, "Oh yeah, that sounds like you're going to get everything just the way you want it . . . but you know," a pause while he squinted at the corral, "you know . . . if you got a bulldozer in there, and knocked that house over right now . . . why, by next spring it'd look real nice after the wildflowers came out."

Millard nodded once at the truth of his suggestion and I had to laugh. His whole delivery was perfect. When I looked at Richard, I was amazed to see him staring at Millard with an expression on his face as if he were incredibly offended. Brautigan wheeled around abruptly and stalked away and Millard went back to watching McGuane's son practice lassoing a sawhorse.

Shortly after this barbeque and the drinking there, Richard's insomnia returned. Then, one morning he announced that, via Stelazine, he had finally got a good night's sleep. Even though I had heard him prowling around the kitchen for most of the night, I believed him because, by then, I wished him any peace of mind—even if it were an illusion.

That afternoon after I came in from work, I ate lunch with Richard, then relaxed on the couch. As we talked I was practicing Italic calligraphy. Richard was pacing around the front room and talking, when suddenly he stopped and asked what I was doing. I told him that I was learning a new art.

"Really?" he said. "Can I see that?"

I handed him the exercise tablet. As was my habit, I wrote down whatever words had the right combination of letters that I needed work on. By chance, some of them had been words from our conversation.

Richard stared down at the pad and apparently located one of his words. He smiled grimly at me and tapped the word before he then carefully tore out both of the worksheets. He handed the blank pad back to me. He folded the sheets in half before tearing them in two and stalking from the room.

It happened so quickly that I was completely nonplussed. The destruction of my practice pages didn't bother me, I was going to throw them away myself, but this sudden outburst of paranoia stunned me.

When he came in the house that evening, he acted as if this scene had never happened, and proceeded to chat about other things. When I made a joke about his search-and-destroy missions for good handwriting—his own was terrible—he was genuinely puzzled. I realized he had experienced a blackout during the episode.

When the jacket copy and bound page proofs for *Sombrero Fallout* arrived, Richard's boredom abated. Apparently he had final say over the jacket copy and enlisted my help in rewriting it.

A couple of evenings were spent listening to Richard as he obsessively wrote and rewrote the description of the novel. What he was trying to find was a way of talking about his work that avoided the 1960 hippie buzz words. He called the project the de-whimsicalizing of his literary reputation.

This notion serves both as a measure of his determination and of his naïveté. Dust jackets don't convince reviewers, and they are certainly ignored by most critics. In Richard's mind he was the only one who could affect this change in the critical climate; he was scornful of the copy Simon & Schuster had sent him.

It was a heroically misguided notion. The novel seemed an unlikely candidate to rescue Brautigan's critical reputation. The story of *Sombrero Fallout* was thin, unreal in an unpleasant way, without engaging characters. The novel was an interesting experiment, combining cartoon violence with a minute account of a failing love affair via a split-screen technique. But with its strained attempts at humor, I judged it unlikely to be a popular book with his fans, either.

I found one detail fascinating, though: in *Sombrero Fallout* the hero, "a humorist," tears up a false start on a story and the pieces of paper go on to have a life of their own, enter reality and start a war. I took this as an artistic recognition by Richard that the public reception of his work was out of his control, something he himself could no longer admit in person.

As we worked on the jacket copy, Brautigan talked about what he was trying to do with his latest novels by combining genres in their subtitles. He called *The Hawkline Monster* a "Gothic Western," *Willard and His Bowling Trophies* "A Perverse Mystery," and *Sombrero Fallout* "A Japanese Novel." It became clear that Richard, with his belief in names—that giving something a label made it that thing—was trying to influence his critics.

Another one of his gambits was shortening the time span of his stories. *Willard* had occured in twenty-four hours and *Fallout* in an hour. He predicted his next novel would take place in the space of a minute. His unspoken hope was these would be seen as tours-de-force and he would be recognized as a virtuoso.

At the same time he was also consciously writing about serious concerns: violence, irrational hate, grief, and loss of innocence via the modern sexual diseases. He was trying to do all this with his usual writing skills: irony, startling metaphors and juxaposition of images. Unfortunately, these genres and themes demanded either psychological characterization or bold dramatic action, neither of which he could use effectively, given his style.

For some writers these novels were interesting and valuable experiments, as Ishmael Reed pointed out in his comments after Brautigan's death. On a more personal level, their techniques mirror Brautigan's state of mind during this difficult time. Marc Chénetier has said his "sentences aspire to autonomy—as if they wanted to ensure their own survival when their surrounding context has collapsed." His sentences became more lapidary and his fictions more fixed in blocks of time with their chapters unmoving moments of attention, statues of prose.

In his art Brautigan could deal with the collapse of meaning that paralleled the waning of his literary stock and his personal "internal strife and tension"—which Chénetier notes is the subject of *Sombrero Fallout.* But in reality Brautigan could not face the fact that his book sales were down and he was losing his popular audience.

From his comments I suspected that his stay in Japan had done the worst possible thing—restored his inflated image of importance as a writer without giving him new material or insights. A friend who accompanied him to Tokyo said he had an audience of top Japanese authors, intellectuals and avant garde artists; in America he had nothing comparable.

This grated on him, even though he regularly scorned any intellectual pronouncements on his work and held most critical writing in contempt. Having won his sudden meteoric rise to fame by the hard work of writing five novels and also by a lot of luck, he felt above any critical apparatus.

One of the things that Montana did give him, with its Hollywood connections, was a sense of transcending what he felt were the limitations of literary business. The film industry saw his work on a popularity and money basis. Since he didn't have critical acceptance, he claimed that he embraced the chance to write screenplays. One night, while working on dust jacket copy, he told me that, with his new Japanese audience, his current screenplay and selling his novels to Hollywood, his goal was now to make a million dollars.

"One million dollars a year," he kept repeating, almost as if hypnotizing himself. "I'm going to make one million dollars in one year."

Taking advantage of Richard's preoccupation with his book, I made an excuse to leave early and arranged for a flight out. Needing someone to oversee the irrigation ditch digging I had set up with a local company, Richard called Price Dunn in California and asked him to fly up and take my place.

Afterwards I was sorry I didn't warn Price about Richard's unstable state of mind. Because they were the oldest of friends, and because Richard always had an immense respect for Price, I thought his benevolent presence would help Richard find some peace. As it turned out, a week later the friendship of over twenty years ended in a scene straight out of a soap opera.

At the Bozeman airport I left the Dodge's car keys at the rental desk for Price, who was flying in that night from San Francisco, along with Richard's new girlfriend. I felt happy to get out. A couple of weeks later, I received a series of grim late night calls from Richard. Price had betrayed him. They could never be friends again. He told me an incoherent story about

Price "abandoning" him at the ranch and destroying the rental car. Richard claimed that this act had "almost wrecked" his friendship with Peter Fonda. It wasn't clear what was going on, only that he was obviously in one of his manic drinking phases again, making late night calls to his friends and detailing his grievances in the monotone he used for such tales.

By some cross referencing with other friends Brautigan had called and by talking to Price in Monterey, I pieced together what had happened. Price hadn't met Richard's new girlfriend, Maria, before this and she turned out to be headstrong and independent. She had caught a ride into Livingston on Friday to do some shopping. When Price drove into town to pick her up at around six that night, he found her at a bar, being entertained by several local cowboys. Price tried to convince her to leave, but she was drunk and her admirers did not want her to leave. Price was not foolish enough to try to argue with a bunch of cowboys on their Friday night out, so he bided his time. He also was not going to call Richard up and tell him his girl was busy honkytonking so they'd be a little late. Another woman in town who fancied Price shanghaied him away for a while. When he returned, Richard's girlfriend had drunk herself out of enough admirers so Price separated her from the remaining hopefuls and sobered her up with coffee for the drive back.

At the ranch Richard was waiting in a jealous rage. He had taken all of Price's clothes out of his room and thrown them on the front lawn. Price and the girl retreated to a neighbor's house and slept there that night. In the morning Price had changed clothes, put the old ones in the trunk of the rental and had absentmindedly left the car keys in his pants pocket. After Richard refused to talk to him, he decided that he had had enough craziness. But the keys were in the trunk now, the car locked, so Price took a cold chisel and knocked a hole in the trunk. Then he drove to the airport, turned in the rental car, and flew back to California. The rental car people billed Peter Fonda for a new trunk. Fonda called Richard in his own rage over the large bill, which Richard paid.

The most revealing thing about the episode was that Richard never admitted his jealousy. In his arrogance he simply could not tolerate the idea that Price could have stolen his girl friend, nor that she might have found life in town more interesting than Chez Brautigan.

When I got back, I noticed that Richard had written, under his signature on the proof copy of *Sombrero Fallout* he gave me in thanks for my work on the dust jacket copy, "Montana Faust." It was an act of such Olympian delusion and hubris that it astounded me. When I told Price of it, he said simply, "Richard's gone insane."

VII. San Francisco
1977-1982

fter the Montana experiences I was wary of being around Richard for any length of time. From reports I was getting from friends, his insomnia and rages were continuing. We discussed how any of us could help him, but the answer was that people had already tried and given up—if they hadn't been exiled by Richard from his life. Erik Weber put it succinctly: "That was the period when Richard was going down his list of friends and knocking them off one by one."

Some regarded the episodes as just more of Richard's eccentricities, but I certainly did not. Psychiatric help was out of the question, since Richard had a horror of shrinks. After his death, it was revealed that he had spent a short time in a mental institution as a young man. This went a long way, for me, in explaining his attitude toward authority. At the time when most of his San Francisco friends were being cut off or slowly squeezed out of his life, his yoyo between Montana and Tokyo began, seeking in the classic alcoholic pattern a geographical solution to his problems.

Sombrero Fallout had not been well received in America, and I knew that this would not help Richard's fragile state of mind. According to his friend Siew-Hwa, he had been working on a screenplay for *The Hawkline Monster,* but that had not gone well, either. He had been asked to rewrite the first draft. Such a request, quite normal for Hollywood practices, was interpreted as rejection by Brautigan. He imperiously cut off all further communications. Siew-Hwa said the producer had sent an assistant up to Montana to negotiate a peace, but Richard had refused to talk any further.

Since he had spent hours telling me over and over how he was going to make a million dollars the next year, refering to a screen deal as the keystone for this notion, I feared that the collapse of this screenwriting project would only make it harder for him to face the situation.

All of this bad news made me uneasy about seeing him, but that fall his agent, Helen Brann, who was also representing me, courtesy of Richard's recommendation, came into town. I was invited to meet her other West Coast clients in her suite at the Stanford Court hotel in San Francisco. When Lani and I arrived, Richard was there, something I wasn't expecting. He had called and told me he would be meeting with her the day before, and didn't think he would stick around. He was looking much like he did up in Montana: drunk, morose and harried. When he was drinking too much, his face tended to go white, even paler than it usually was, and that night he looked like a corpse.

There were a few other writers in the room, and after the introductions, Lani and I settled down to chat with them and find out what everyone was doing. One was the journalist John Grissam, who was working on a book on jealousy, in collaboration with Dr. Eugene Schoenfeld, writer of the underground press medical advice column, Dr. Hip. Since the book was going to be an anthology of interviews, Grissam asked each of us about our experiences with jealousy.

During this discussion, Richard hovered around the edge of the group, disappearing from time to the time into the other room of the suite to make phone calls. Apparently he was due somewhere else but had not made connections.

As the evening progressed, it was clear that Grissam admired Brautigan's work. From his comments he seemed fascinated with what he imagined was the freedom of being a rich and famous writer. He made several remarks to Richard about this. Each time Richard deflected the inquiries with one of his usual oblique monotone replies.

But Grissam was so earnest about it all, Richard sat down on the carpet next to him and began to talk about the effect of fame on writers. It was not really a discussion, because no matter what Grissam asserted, Richard kept insisting that fame was in itself meaningless, that only the work mattered. If you continued to write good work, then fame was the kicker, sometimes good and sometimes bad. But it counted for nothing in relation to the real work of writing.

Grissam's persistence in believing that fame was a boon for a writer soon exasperated Richard. By this time he had drunk too much whiskey, and I saw that he was about to explode. At one point, when the conversation turned to the money that fame could bestow, Richard erupted. He stood up in a rage, tore up some twenty dollar bills, and rained them down on Grissam. "This isn't real. You think this is real?" Richard said. "This is nothing."

Then in his rage he fell to his knees on the carpet and grabbed one of Grissam's legs around the calf and pounded his foot on the floor. "This leg is more real than any of that," Richard said.

He abruptly bolted into the next room, leaving everyone stunned. After conversations resumed and everyone regained their composure, including Grissam, Richard came back with a fresh tumbler of whiskey and stood in the hallway.

After Grissam checked to see if Richard was still manic, he began telling quietly why he was writing the book on jealousy. He had been very much in love with someone and had been treated badly. In his rage over this, something had gone haywire in his body. His leg had mysteriously atrophied. Unable to get help from any western medicine, he had gone to various other countries and tried different cures, paying for them by writing articles on each treatment. Pulling up his pants leg, he showed us the damage. It was the leg which Richard had pounded on the floor. Pointing to his leg, he said Richard was right, this is more real than any of that other stuff.

Brautigan was moved by this and became very contrite and soliticious of Grissam. He sat down on the carpet and apologized for his outburst. Shortly after that he got his phone call and left.

The look on his face as he heard about Grissam's leg was

heart-rending. Even though he was drunk, his face almost white from whiskey, Richard had gone intuitively to the source of another person's pain.

That night Lani and I had a long discussion about the episode. Very depressed, I couldn't help but think this instinct to be a curse. I knew Richard was lost in a way most people never understand. With his belief in intuition and emotion, Richard was doomed to return constantly to his own pain, and just as doomed to rehearse it without relief. He could not cure himself because his art could give him no relief and yet it would never let him be.

Even after my experiences in Montana, until that night I still hoped that there would be a way out for Richard, that his situation was only temporary. But what I had seen that night seemed so final, and so terrible, hope no longer seemed possible.

I had the feeling that nothing could help Richard now. His mind had turned in on itself, and slowly rage was becoming the energy for his imagination. Previously Brautigan had used his imagination to free himself from his history, from the quirk of fate that gave him a role as the abused child and social geek. Richard saw the world as populated with dead things, and the past a marble replica of breathing life. What sincerely perplexed him was how other people could worship these. He poked fun at such delusions, with a playful, Buddhist vision of the transitoriness of things. When he was vaulted into the ranks of the Haves, he was drawn to people like Tom McGuane and his vision of life. Brautigan loved to describe a scene from McGuane's movie *Rancho Deluxe*, where the heroes shoot holes in a Lincoln Continental. But the shooting wasn't done with just any gun. A .50 caliber Sharps was used, the principal weapon for the extermination of the buffalo. In his love of stylish gestures, Brautigan wanted to flaunt a symbolic disdain for material things, ignoring that after all, a bullet hole is only a bullet hole. Yet while he claimed not to rely on the good life, he loved the perks of fame once he saw how they glorified his self-image. To wake up from this dream, with a possible return to the poverty of his earlier life, terrified him as much as these fascination with his own ruin drew him on.

His attitudes were similiar to those Mark Twain experienced late in his life. Twain was enraged and disgusted with the state of society and with himself for his debt-ridden and money-grubbing situation, until the death of his daughter shocked him back to reality. Feeling as if he had been wakened from a bad dream, he had called his attitude "The Devil's Race Track"— delusion and anger circling out of control in his mind. I couldn't imagine what shock could free Richard from his turmoil.

After the incident in the Stanford Court, I saw Richard infrequently. I knew he had two periods of calm during that time, when he seemed like the person I used to know. The first was some months later. Richard returned from Tokyo with a broken nose. When he described how this happened, he quite frankly said that he was badmouthing someone (he used the phrase "running them down viciously"). A man sitting next to him, whom he didn't know, had turned around and flattened him, breaking his nose. This rude and deserved punishment seemed to bring Richard back into the real world for a time. He actually inquired about my life, seemed interested in my replies, and acted as if he cared. Valerie Estes took advantage of this calm to chastise him for his extreme self-centeredness. For a time after that Richard took care to open himself to other people's situations, being considerate and kind in a way that reminded me of his younger days.

His marriage in 1977 to a Japanese woman, Akiko, also seemed to help him at first. Most of the personal, though often solipsistic stories in *The Tokyo-Montana Express* were written while she was with him. Some of the burdens of coping with everyday life lifted, he had a euphoric relaxed attitude and was pleasant to be around.

Although I hoped for the best, his romantic misogyny made it difficult to see how any of his relationships could last. He loved to be in love with women, but feared them when the romance was over. Because of his severe problems with control, none of his friends held out much hope for this union.

As one woman said to me, with malice, "Wait until his wife learns to speak English."

Once the marriage soured, Richard became more and more alcoholic and depressed. His isolation increased, as did his late night phone calls, recounting over and over, as if his memory were gone, details of his impending divorce. Fueled by Calvados, the monologues were unbearable.

During this time Richard told me, "I guess the only thing I can do is write. If that's so, then that's all I'll do." He seemed to be saying that he was going to forego any other contacts with people. I think that he did just that, and that it helped to kill his spirit. Writing alone cannot sustain a man, but in his willfulness, Richard thought it could.

My last face-to-face contact with Richard occurred after *The Tokyo-Montana Express* was published. He was determined to hustle the book and make back the money he felt he was going to lose on his divorce settlement. When he got back from the first swing of his promotion tour, reading at various western colleges, he was dismayed at how badly his audience had shrunk. He found that he was no longer even known by young readers. "They don't read," was what he said, but what he really meant was that they no longer read him.

I hoped that by returning to the business of being a writer, his book promotions would occupy him and lessen his pain. He seemed so determined to rescue his reputation and his audience that I imagined he could make a comeback, perhaps even healing himself in doing so. Certainly he was going through a recognition that he had been addicted to fame—not just the money, but the heady adulation. Perhaps he could come to some kind of realistic reassessment of his situation on his reading tour. *The Toyko-Montana Express* was also getting good reviews and had been picked up by a book club. All this, I felt, would contribute to his recovery.

A few months after the book party for *The Tokyo-Montana Express,* Richard returned from his East Coast tour, which he thought was successful. We were at Enrico's, and he turned to me, apropos of nothing, and said, "You know, there are two people I wouldn't ever fight: you and Tom McGuane."

Now, when a friend tells you that, he has been thinking about the possiblity. I began to realize what he was really telling me. Richard had been exhibiting such contrary and contradictory behavoir that I knew it was only a matter of time. Unnerved by this, and very sad, I got up immediately and left the restaurant. That was the last time I saw him. A few months later I heard that he and Tom had been in a feud and were no longer speaking.

In his last published book, *So The Wind Won't Blow It All Away*, Brautigan had again tried to deal directly with his childhood. I found a possible reason for that incident with the .22 rifle in Montana. In a strangely disjointed narrative, the book's teen-age protagonist relates how he accidentally shot and killed a friend while out plinking. Had this adolescent trauma—whether real or imagined, no one close to Richard seems to know—haunted him all his life? After his death I talked to Ianthe, but she had no knowledge of any such incident. But in talking to an old Monterey friend, Michael Sowl, we both recalled an evening with Price Dunn when Brautigan told a story of shooting at some apples out of an attic window with a .22 and hitting someone miles away. Whether that person died or was only wounded, neither of us could remember. Neither of us knew whether Brautigan told this story about himself or about someone else.

Reading the novel, I noticed another sign that he was in the worst shape of his life. For the first time I could recall, I saw many clumsy and badly written sentences. He'd written bad fiction before, but usually his sentences stayed concise and clear. Although the story was interesting, his timing was off, something that had never occurred even in his thinnest work; he always told the flattest jokes quite crisply. The prose seemed truly lost and meandering. In a memoir of Brautigan published in the magazine *Rolling Stock*, a Montana friend spoke of the novel's "sixty-word sentences." That meticulous phrase I am sure echoes Richard's voice, maintaining that a triumph in writing long sentences would impress the reviewers and shed, once and for all, the critical disdain for his simple sentences and bare plots. Style would save his career.

In a radio broadcast Don Carpenter commented that *So The Wind Won't Blow It All Away* was the one book that Richard did not send him. When Don asked him about it, Richard claimed it was a mistake, but Carpenter didn't think so. I think he was right. Richard was aware how badly his prose—something he took fierce pride in—was slipping.

Sporadic calls from Richard continued, but whenever he phoned, it was as if he were drunkenly playing a tape of the last conversation we had, constantly referring to his status in Japan and lack of it here. His anger, his bitter self-imposed isolation, were magnified by his now unrelenting arrogance.

While he was aware of what he was doing, he was helpless to change it. According to Carpenter, Richard's self-image had plummeted when he contracted herpes sometime in the late seventies. His loathing for his physical deterioration surfaced in an unpublished short story from around 1979, "What The Mad Scientist Has Left Behind." It begins as a meditation on aging, but the story ends with this sentence, "What mad scientist in his diabolical laboratory created this monster that has become me?"

Compulsively in need of friends, he was just as compulsive now about abusing them. From his German translator, Günter Ohnemus, I received a report that during his European trip in 1983 Brautigan was out of control. He had skipped or trashed readings, and had fired his agent. He made the bizarre claim that a computer in a Tokyo hotel was going to handle all his writing business. Günter also said that Richard botched deals and had lost the chance to make a considerable amount of money while in Europe.

Even though his death by drink or misadventure seemed inevitable to me, I didn't think he would kill himself. I couldn't imagine him doing that because he was so stubborn and willful about surviving. Only after his death did Siew-Hwa tell me about his constant references to suicide during their time together, always threatening to do it with a gun.

Bobbie Louise Hawkins saw him shortly before his death and

she thought his shooting was an accident. She hypothesized that Brautigan was playing at suicide during a drunken depression, perhaps over not writing. I can't agree. From the evidence in the archive, he was writing both poetry and prose until his death. From other reports of his last days in Bolinas and San Francisco, a pattern emerges. Even as loopy as Richard was in his last years, he was still willful and precise in certain areas under his control. I think he planned his suicide. His friend, the private detective David Fechheimer, had that same sense. "I think he'd decided to do it [a year before]. He was more at peace during the summer [of 1984], like he'd passed a hurdle."

Evidence in the papers found by his body indicates this, too. Several poems are meditations on karma and reincarnation. This one was untitled.

Somehow we live and die again,
I wonder why to me it just seems
   another beginning.
Everything leads to something else, so
   I think I'll start
      over again.
Maybe I'll learn something new
Maybe I won't
Maybe it will just be the same
   beginning again
Time goes fast
   for no reason
Because it all starts
   over again
I'm not going anyplace
except where I've
   been before.

Two particular poems, written on a Japanese hotel's stationery, may give a sense of his decision to commit suicide. The first is called "Reflection."

God, all the shit
that is going to be written
    about me
after I am dead.
                    —Tokyo, 2/10/84

The second poem "Death Growth," dated two days later, is
more chilling.

There was a darkness
upon the darkness,
and only the death
    growth
was growing. It
grew like
the darkness upon darkness
    growing.

In his anger against the world for the withdrawal of acclaim, an
acclaim he might secretly have believed was unearned, I think
he planned for his body not to be discovered. So many of his
gestures in those last years, from all reports, were so spiteful
and angry that it fits into Richard's rage.

"I think Richard was angry and out of money and
goddamned if he was going to take a cut in pay," Carpenter
said. "I think it was a coldly rational kind of act. I could hear
him saying, 'Everyone thought I was going to go down begging
for my crust, but fuck 'em. Now I don't have to answer my
telephone.' "

On September 14, Brautigan was in North Beach and he ran
into his ex-wife Aki. He refused to talk to her and she said, "He
closed his eyes as if he saw a ghost." Later that day, he told
Marcia Clay, "I feel like my whole life has happened to me in
one day." Before going back to Bolinas, he borrowed a pistol
from a San Francisco restaurant owner, Jimmy Sakata. Calls to
his house were met by the answering machine. Slowly the
batteries ran down and his voice got slower and slower until
the tape stopped altogether.

The night of October 26 when his body was discovered (but the suicide still unannounced), I talked to some of his friends in San Francisco, trying to find out what had gone on while he was in the city. Not much was known. Several only knew that Richard had told them not to come looking for him in Bolinas, since he was definitely returning to Montana. Two people said they went over on the chance that he had not left, but found the house dark. The fact that he carefully told Becky Fonda in Montana that he was not returning indicates the design for his suicide. And his last act before leaving Montana—giving Tom McGuane a wrapped package containing a funeral urn and telling him he'd have instructions when this was needed— can't be more clear. While in Bolinas, Brautigan made a phone call to a book dealer about selling off his manuscripts, claiming that he wanted to set up a trust fund for his daughter. This act could merely have indicated how desperate and broke he was, but I think it was Richard's attempt to clean things up before he died.

Marcia Clay's journal about Brautigan's last days, quoted in the *Rolling Stone* article, reveals more about his preparation for suicide. On his last phone call to her from Bolinas, Brautigan asked Marcia if she liked his mind and this question reads as a self-pitying taunt, because it was a mind he was about to destroy. It's my belief that, in his anger and desolation, Richard wanted his remains to waste away in that gloomy Bolinas house, as a final comment on his regard for the world.

On Brautigan's overriding willfulness, Michael McClure commented, "His self-killing was a culmination of the awkward kid's triumph over both his enemies and friends. Right out of the nowhere of the Depression-ridden Pacific Northwest he'd surfaced and triumphed and ruined himself. What was left?"

Someone should have been able to help him, but most of his friends had to admit that they had already tried and failed. His suicide provided his friends with a sober reflection on the powers and deficiencies of friendship. A sense of helplessness compounds the grief.

I don't think it's fair to Brautigan to end this memoir here, because I don't think of him in terms of his death. When I remember Richard, I like to see him in San Francisco when he lived on Union Street and he was the active, generous and funny friend to so many people in North Beach. His flat was a spacious and sunny meeting place where we started on our daily adventures. His was a miraculous and freewheeling life, and he was sailing through it with a gentle and cheerful grace.

Often we'd spend the day knocking around town. Usually we'd end up with a few friends in some restaurant for dinner, drinks and a lot of laughing and goofing around. One particular anecdote comes to mind to illustrate Richard's best side.

After the Christmas holidays, Brautigan called me up. "I'm back in town. Why don't we get together some afternoon for a drink?"

I said sure and we made a date. When I met him at Enrico's, he was at an outdoor table, looking bright-eyed and expectant, radiating a mischievous, infectious energy.

"What's up with you?" I asked.

"We've got a little work to do first, before we eat."

"No hurry."

"We'll have lunch at Vanessi's after we're done with the work."

"Fine. What are we going to do?"

"A friend of mine is about to finish a book he's been working on for years. He's having some problems," Richard said. "We have to wait for a carpenter."

I didn't ask why a carpenter. Richard was enjoying his secret too much to ruin it with a question. We waited and over a few cups of coffee we shoptalked literary news. After a while, a carpenter walked across Broadway with his tool box in hand and came toward our table.

"Here he is."

We got up and met him on the sidewalk. Nothing much was said because the carpenter seemed to know what the story was. He only nodded at us, and Richard nodded back. We walked down Broadway past the strip joints and entered a doorway. The words SAN FRANCISCO HOTEL were in gold letters across the glass door. We entered a narrow lobby and climbed some stairs. Behind us, the carpenter's tool box went *chick-chick-chick* as his tools joggled around.

At the top of the stairs was a door with a wire cage inset in the upper half. Behind the wire was a dead man, posing as the desk clerk. His open eyes stared straight ahead.

"We're going to fix room 16," Richard said to the desk clerk. He waited for a reaction, but there wasn't any, so Brautigan continued climbing the stairs. The carpenter and I followed. The dead man's eyes didn't move as we filed past. He didn't even blink at the *chick-chick-chick* sounds.

When we reached the top of the stairs, we turned down a yellow hallway. At the end of the hallway was a grey dirty window overlooking Broadway, and beside it a green door. Pasted on it in cheap silver dayglo decals were the numbers 1 and 6.

Below those was a ragged hole. The door was a plywood model, and someone had taken a great deal of effort and kicked a hole through the middle. Around the lock were three overlapping reinforced areas, the bottom one of plywood, the second one of solid board and top layer of tin. The door had been jimmied and beaten and smashed. At the bottom, below the new hole, there was a sheet of aluminum, dented and pitted with kicks. During its lifetime that door had caused a lot of trouble.

Richard reached through the hole in the door and undid the lock from the inside. The door swung open and Richard stepped aside to let the carpenter in.

"My friend can't come back to the hotel until the door is fixed," he explained.

"It's hard to fix a door if they won't let you back in the building," the carpenter said, setting his tool box down on the floor. "You did right by calling me." The carpenter opened the tool box, took out a tape and measured the hole.

I stepped into the room behind him. I expected a mess, but the room was extremely neat. The bed was made. The floor was clean. The room was tiny, but everything was in its place. By the window was a small table with an Olympia portable on top. A chair was pushed under the table. In front of the typewriter were stacks of typing paper boxes, six in all. One held a manuscript, face down. A waterglass contained pens and pencils. A *Roget's Thesaurus* and a worn two-volume set of the *Shorter Oxford English Dictionary* leaned against the wall.

I looked into a wastebasket alongside of the table. Manuscript pages were piled up, each sheet torn into four equal pieces. The room was stunning in its perfection. Coming into that hotel room from the hall was like going from a war zone into a religious shrine.

"I've got a piece of plywood in my truck that'll fix this. It'll take about an hour," the carpenter said. He put away his measuring tape, reached down in the waste basket and took out a quarter of a discarded manuscript page, ruining the perfect symmetry of the room. He turned the paper over on its blank side and wrote down two numbers. "I won't need any help getting the plywood, so you can go if you want. The guy lost his key, huh?"

"Yeah. He was coming back from doing some last piece of research for his novel," Richard explained. "He really wanted to get back to his book. But it was the second night in a row that he had lost his key. The management didn't have a second spare. He really wanted to get typing again and finish his novel."

No one said anything about the dead desk clerk in the cage and how difficult it must have been to convince him to go get a new key made.

"When you're done fixing the door, come back to Enrico's. I'll pay you there."

We left the room and started down the stairs. On the way past the cage I looked in. A television was now sitting on the chair where the clerk had been. The dead man had been replaced by a small Japanese television set. Automation had come to the San Francisco Hotel.

When Richard and I returned to Enrico's, a man at the corner table stood up. His head was shaved. For a second, I thought he was wearing make-up because of the large magenta smear above his left eye. But then I looked closer and saw that the smear was a bruise about the size of an elongated plum. Inside it little black stitches posed as his left eyebrow.

Richard went over and talked to the man with the bruise. While the man listened, he stood nodding, then he shook hands with Richard, and drifted out onto Broadway. Richard came back inside to our table.

"What happened to him?"

"Candelabra."

"He got hit with a candlestick?"

"Yeah. A silver one. After he got done with the second to the last chapter on his novel, he decided to celebrate. When he came back to the room to finish his novel, he couldn't get in and busted down the door and got thrown out of his hotel."

A waiter came over. Our work day done, we ordered two white wines. Richard continued the saga. "He's an old newspaper man so he ended up with an old friend of his in a press club here in town. That night they flew down to San Diego on some assignment. My friend was arrested in Tijuana for shooting out windows with a CO_2 pistol and spent Christmas Eve in the Tijuana jail."

At this juncture, Richard paused, to let me take my time imagining what the Tijuana jail must have been like on Christmas Eve.

"When he got back to San Francisco, he went to a fancy New Year's Eve party so he could borrow some money and fix the door and finish his novel. He was hustling the tables for bread and he said the wrong thing to a black football player there and the guy hit him with the candelabra."

The waiter brought our white wines and placed them on the table. Richard paused until he left before starting again.

"My friend said he was lucky. The doctor on duty at the hospital emergency ward that night happened to be a cosmetic surgeon."

"He did a real nice job on the cut," I observed.

"Didn't he? My friend says once the eyebrow grows back, you'll hardly notice the scar."

We raised our wine glasses. "Here's to that last chapter," Richard toasted. "It better be good."

VIII. Shadows and Marble

"What I desired to do in marble,
I can poke my shadow through."
—Richard Brautigan
(from an unpublished short story,
"The F. Scott Fitzgerald Ahhhhhhhhhhh, Pt. 2")

S ince Richard Brautigan's death, his reputation has hardly been cast in marble. His writing has been relegated to the shadowland of popular flashes, that peculiar American graveyard of overnight sensations. When a writer dies, appreciation of his work seldom reverses field, but continues in the direction that it was headed at the moment of death, and this has been true for Brautigan. Even during Brautigan's bestseller years in the United States, critical studies of his work were few. Those there were never exerted a strong influence on the chiefs of the American critical establishment.

As both a popular and a West Coast writer, his work has been easy to ignore. There are no critical journals on the West Coast which can sustain a writer's career, as there are in the East. His popularity among the young dumped his work with literary lightweights, such as Richard Bach or Eric Segal, and counter-culture fads as Abbie Hoffman, Jerry Rubin, or Charles Reich.

Curiously, a critical climate of open hostility to Brautigan's work prevailed on the eastern seaboard and his work was perceived as a threat. From the first it was an object of ridicule, receiving much the same treatment as Jack Kerouac's novels did in the 1950s. Brautigan's literary position for his generation also was similiar to the one Kerouac provided for the Beats: Brautigan became the most famous novelist for a social movement whose literary constituency were almost solely poets. Speaking politically, most poets have little recourse to effective

147

literary power, lacking steady income, steady publication and/ or reviewing positions. Brautigan did not have the safety of a group of novelists or a regular circle of reviewers friendly to his aesthetics; consequently, he had few defenders. Brautigan did not write reviews himself, or even issue manifestos. He was perceived as the stray, and so to attack his work risked no reply. In the *Vanity Fair* article published after Brautigan's death, the playwright and poet Michael McClure acknowledged this hostility and offered this re-evaluation: "His wasn't a dangerous voice so much as a voice of diversity, potentially liberating in that it showed the possiblities of dreaming, of beauty and the playfulness of the imagination."

With the burden of a ridiculed sociological movement attached to his work, positive literary criticism was sparse. Often what commentary there was tried to talk about both the hippie community and Brautigan's fiction, and failed at both. Ironically, his first four novels were written before the hippie phenomenon, and the relationship between the two was an accident of chronology at first, and then a media cliché.

While his prolific output generated plentiful newspaper reviews, these usually functioned as simple indicators of his perceived fame. Most echoed previous prejudice that he was a whimsical writer for cultural dropouts, and neither his writing nor his supposed subjects were to be considered important. What has to be remembered about criticism is that even serious critics seldom create much lasting literature themselves, and most newspaper reviewers are inevitably trafficking in fishwrap.

The true test of a creative writer is whether the literature is remembered by good writers and begets more excellent work. Other authors have acknowledged Brautigan's influence. Ishmael Reed applauded Brautigan's courage in experimenting with genres in his later novels and claimed this had an effect on his own experimental and highly acclaimed novels of the 1970s. In 1985, the popular and respected novelist W.P. Kinsella published *The Alligator Report,* containing short stories which he dubbed "Brautigans." In his foreword he spoke of how this work arose directly from Brautigan's fictional strategies, stating

"I can't think of another writer who has influenced my life and career as much."

The spare early stories of Raymond Carver have always shown a strong connection, stylistically and culturally, to Brautigan's first two novels and short stories. Both writers create a similiar West Coast landscape of unemployed men, dreaming women, or failed artists trapped in domestic and economic limbos while attempting to maintain their distinctly Western myths of self-sufficient individuality.

Implicit in most negative criticism of Brautigan is the charge that he wrote fantasies about cultural aberrations, such as the hippies, with little connection to important levels of American life. I think this is mistaken. A strong cultural reality can be found in his work, that of people on the bottom rungs of American society, living out their unnoticed and idiosyncratic existences. Traditionally, this class has been one of the resources for American literature. While discussing *Huckleberry Finn*, V.S. Pritchett writes that one of America's cultural heroes is "a natural anarchist and bum" and called the book "the first of those typical American portraits of the underdog, which have culminated in the poor white literature...." Many of Brautigan's works are rooted in this underclass and his people are, in Pritchett's words, the "underdog who gets along on horse sense."

It is often the fate of writers about American popular culture to find an audience in foreign countries. Faulkner's work was out-of-print here in the early 1940s but revered in France. Henry Miller and Charles Bukowski are two other examples. During his lifetime, Brautigan's writing was translated into seventeen languages. His work commands international respect and continues to generate comment. In Japan, where twelve of his books have been translated, he is considered an important American writer. (And it is of interest that Carver's fiction now enjoys an equally high level of popularity in Japan.) West Germany continues to publish his work and a television documentary on him is under way. In France, Marc Chénetier's book-length study was published with accompanying translations of three Brautigan novels. This critical work was later translated into English as part of Methuen's excellent Contemporary Writers series.

In America of the 1980s, Brautigan's work is treated as only an object for nostalgia, and confined to rehashes of the love generation. When roll-calls of fictional innovators are published in critical articles, his name has been dropped from the list of Ishmael Reed, John Barth, Donald Barthelme, Robert Coover, and others.

Brautigan's work remains the best way we have to regard him, other than as an historical figure. I have to think the work is what really matters. Whatever follies, sins or beauties a writer possesses, they are secondary considerations to the complete body of writing.

In the following pages, I'll cover what I see as the virtues of Brautigan's work. Because his unique style is what most readers notice and enjoy first, I'll start with that, discuss his first two novels, and then go on to his themes and demonstrate how his style works with them.

In a useful observation on Brautigan's poetry, Robert Creeley commented,

> I don't think Richard is interested in so-called melopoeia, he said he wants to say things using the simplest possible unit of statement as the module.

Simple sentences and minimal rhythms occur in Brautigan's fiction, too, but they work with his metaphors to obtain a more complex effect than in his poetry. By controlling the colloquial sound of his prose, Brautigan developed a strategy for releasing emotion while utilizing the anarchic and comical responses of his imagination.

"The Kool-Aid Wino" chapter in *Trout Fishing in America* provides an example of this strategy.

> When I was a child I had a friend who became a Kool-Aid wino as the result of a rupture. He was a member of a very large and poor German family. All the older

children in the family had to work in the field during
the summer, picking beans for two-and-one-half cents
a pound to keep the family going. Everyone worked
except my friend who couldn't because he was
ruptured. There was no money for an operation. There
wasn't even enough money to buy him a truss. So he
stayed home and became a Kool-Aid wino.

What can be said about this? First, except for the fanciful
notion of a Kool-Aid wino, this paragraph has the sound of the
English plain style. Brautigan wrote in a colloquial voice, but
sometimes it had a curiously unmelodic and muted quality.
The voice sounded as if the speaker were talking, but not
always consciously aware of being heard. This might account
for what other people have dubbed the naive quality of
Brautigan's fiction: the tone of a child talking to himself. And for
all his colloquial rhythms, slang or common nursery rhyme
devices, such as alliteration and internal rhyme, are carefully
rationed, because both require that the reader hear them. In the
paragraph, two incongruous states, being ruptured and being a
wino, are joined, but the last has a rider attached, modifying it
with a fairy-tale quality of special powers derived from
common objects.

One morning in August I went over to his house. He
was still in bed. He looked up at me from underneath
a tattered revolution of old blankets. He had never
slept under a sheet in his life.
"Did you bring the nickel you promised?" he asked.
"Yeah," I said. "It's here in my pocket."
"Good."

While the scene is being set, Brautigan slips in the metaphor
of the blankets, but in a sentence which has the similar declar-
ative rhythm as the sentences just before and after it. This
blanket metaphor sounds no more important or remarkable
rhythmically than the lack of an operation or the absence of a

truss, but the metaphor is, in this context, spectacularly surreal.

He also used very little rhythmic speech in his dialogue. Often his dialogue is even more uninflected than his narrative passages. As Tom McGuane wrote, "His dialogue is supernaturally exact. . . ." Muting rhythm in dialogue and in narrative passages dampens the emotional content. This has an interesting effect because hearing a voice calls for a much more emotional reaction than silent narrative passages. This is why "dialect" novels are so exhausting to read. They require much more concentration and emotional response. First-person narrative calls for more effort from the reader than third person because we are listening and responding to one person. Brautigan often got a third person objectivity while writing in first person.

His strategy was to control and minimize the reader's responses until he was ready to tap into them. In both his dialogue and narrative, he habitually tried for emotionally neutral sentences. While still maintaining a colloquial tone, the narrative sentences sound normal, the dialogue sounds minimally conversational, so they may slide by unchallenged by a reader's emotional response. What is crucial to Brautigan's style is that both dialogue and narrative strike a similiar sound and a neutral equality is created between them.

Once Brautigan establishes this pattern in a work, then simple statements of fact can be followed by a simple sentence bearing a fantastic and imaginative statement. The strategy is, accept A, accept B, therefore accept off-the-wall C. The poet Philip Whalen explained the effect of Brautigan's style this way: ". . . in Brautigan for example complete clarity and complete exact use of words and at the same time this lunatic imagination and excitement all going 100 miles an hour. . . ."

To change to a biological metaphor, what happens in Brautigan's prose is that the parasitical imagination invades and occupies the host of precise, orderly prose, subverting, disrupting and eventually usurping the factual prose's function.

He was careful to see that the jar did not overflow and

the precious Kool-Aid spill out onto the ground. When the jar was full he turned the water off with a sudden but delicate motion like a famous brain surgeon removing a disordered portion of the imagination. Then he screwed the lid tightly onto the top of the jar and gave it a good shake.

To give a realistic base for his fiction, Brautigan often started with mundane social situations and built from there, carefully placing one rhythmically neutral sentence on top of another. This lulls the reader into a false sense of security, and a false sense of security is a good first step for comic writing. In doing this, Brautigan sensed the emotional vibrations that are inevitable in the simplest sentences, so he could then upset them and introduce that lovely sense of comic panic.

Of course, there is a problem with this strategy. No matter how short, factual, or laconic sentences may be, writing always carries some shade of voice. The human voice resonates feeling and Brautigan knew this. By creating a kind of equal neutrality between factual sound and fanciful content through the use of similiar sentence structures, he tried to return to a realistic narrative, once he had disrupted it with metaphors. At times he simply alternated between the two, giving the fantastic equal time with the mundane.

"Hello," said the grocer. He was bald with a red birthmark on his head. The birthmark looked just like an old car parked on his head. He automatically reached for a package of grape Kool-Aid and put it on the counter.

"Five cents."

"He's got it."

I reached into my pocket and gave the nickel to the grocer. He nodded and the old red car wobbled back and forth on the road as if the driver were having an epileptic seizure.

Or, at times, he would let the metaphor grow from a single

sentence about a commonplace, until it took over the paragraph. In this example from *A Confederate General*, the rhythm speeds up as the metaphor expands.

> Night was coming on in, borrowing the light. It had started out borrowing just a few cents worth of the light, but now it was borrowing thousands of dollars worth of the light every second. The light would soon be gone, the bank closed, the tellers unemployed, the bank president a suicide.

Fiction must have drama, however minimal, but given this strategy in Brautigan's prose, often the drama is on the surface of the writing itself. The tension between the two poles of Brautigan's style, the plain and the metaphorical, creates the conflict in his fiction. In the passage quoted above, the first person character/narrator is so hyped up about visiting his eccentric Kool-Aid wino friend and witnessing his rituals that his imagination runs wild. But no one in the story notices this, so this potential conflict is confined to the prose itself. Just as the "I" character remains undercover in the mundane tale of buying Kool-Aid, the fantasy remains undercover in a plain prose.

Brautigan's writing has been called undramatic, because in a conventional sense it is. His style provides what drama there is more often than his characters. His metaphors function as dramatic resolutions, if subversion of common reality by imaginative thought can be called a resolution. (One of Brautigan's themes is that ultimately this strategy subverts and disrupts the very act of writing fiction.) The fanciful notion of a Kool-Aid wino provides the impetus to continue reading, not any drama between the characters. The Kool-Aid Wino will nowhere insist on the strangeness of his behavior, while the narrator will provide the tension with his perceptions of that behavoir as being very special in a magical world. Often the rhythms do not insist that this is a special occasion any more than does the Kool-Aid wino. The sentences chart a rather unremarkable exchange between the two characters but this exchange is seen by a quite metaphorical intelligence, and so the prose itself enacts the eventual theme of the piece, that illumination comes from within.

He created his own Kool-Aid reality and was able to illuminate himself by it.

Besides a plain, slightly colloquial style, Brautigan also favored a factual structure to give a neutral tone to his sentences. Facts are meant to be understood, not heard and savored on their own. Brautigan loved to infiltrate and sabotage them. Here's an example from the opening chapter of *A Confederate General.*

I've heard that the population of Big Sur in those Civil War days was mostly just some Digger Indians. I've heard that the Digger Indians down there didn't wear any clothes. They didn't have any fire or shelter or culture. They didn't grow anything. They didn't hunt and they didn't fish. They didn't bury their dead or give birth to their children. They lived on roots and limpets and sat pleasantly out in the rain.

During this masquerade of historical prose, the manipulation of a catalogue style develops a strange emotional equivalency between the sentences which their content quietly disrupts. One source of this technique comes from the Western tall-tale, where a narrator, disguised as an expert, mixes the fantastic with the normal in equal portions. This passage reminds me of Twain in his role as the seasoned traveler in *A Tramp Abroad.*

The table d'hôte was served by waitresses dressed in the quaint and comely costume of the Swiss peasant. This consists of a simple gros de laine trimmed with ashes of roses with overskirt of sacre blue ventre saint gris, cut bias on the off-side, with facings of petit polanaise and narrow insertions of pâté de foie gras backstitched to the mise en scène in the form of a *jeu d'espirit.* It gives the wearer a singularly piquant and alluring aspect.

In both Twain's and Brautigan's paragraphs, anarchy is hatched inside the standardized English. Twain's prose has the trotting rhythm of standard fill-in-the-blanks travel or fashion writing. Brautigan's prose creates his bland rhythms through the careful alternation of "ands" and "ors" in factual sentences designed to be read and forgotten. Twain's intent is burlesque, and Brautigan's opts for a quieter anarchy. But the strategies for both seem similar.

A more complicated example of Brautigan's technique with this factual sound can be found in his short story, "Pacific Radio Fire." The opening paragraph begins:

The largest ocean in the world starts or ends at Monterey, California.

There's no sense of who is saying this. Since the story title has a radio in it, the voice could be someone on the radio, but it doesn't have to be, it could be anybody. Then Brautigan adds the next fact.

It depends on what language you are speaking.

These two statements are acceptable, reasonable, and dispassionate. Nothing in their rhythm seems emotional or unusual. Put them together and they enact only a slightly different way of viewing the universe.

The largest ocean in the world starts or ends at Monterey, California. It depends on what language you are speaking.

However one thing has changed. With the use of "you," the reader is now addressed, and his presence is acknowledged, giving a slightly more colloquial edge to the second sentence than the first, an intimacy. Then the third sentence plunges us into an emotional, very intimate situation—but without any corresponding passionate rhythm.

> The largest ocean in the world starts or ends at Monterey, California. It depends on what language you are speaking. My friend's wife had just left him.

Now, these three sentences present a fact followed by another fact followed by third fact, but the last one is wildly removed from the reality of the first two. More importantly, the third sentence is colloquially factual. The first two have the tone of the mundane media facts that wash over us daily, while the third sentence belongs to the everyday world of emotional distress. The third sentence is something that any private person could say, just as any public commentator could say the first two.

This sequence establishes what I call neutral equality among the three sentences. The shift cracks the emotionless facade that the paragraph starts with and abruptly releases humor. While the language remains low-key, its arrangement yields the drama.

This linguistic shift is also curiously realistic, and I mean realistic in the manner that these verbal traumas occur. To my ear, this shift mimes the kind of dislocations that result when someone is trying to tell you how something bad happened, but doesn't know how to start. Instead they talk about the weather, the scenery, and then suddenly blurt out their distress without any rhythmic or emotional buildup. A familiar "out-of-the-blue" quality to the rapid shift from impersonal to personal occurs. Here it works as comic timing.

> The largest ocean in the world starts or ends at Monterey, California. It depends on what language you are speaking. My friend's wife had just left him. She

walked right out the door and didn't even say goodbye. We went and got two fifths of port and headed for the Pacific.

What makes this more than a mere joke is that there is a vibration set off by the word "language" in the second sentence and the fact that the wife left without using any language. Brautigan at his best discovers a taut, underground humor in his prose by suppressing connections that other writers might make obvious. Someone else might have written, "and didn't even use language to say goodbye." One of the strengths of his style is that he leaves the right things unsaid and trusts the placement of his language to supply the emotion.

When Brautigan tried to reverse this progression, going from the colloquial emotional truth to the dry facts, from the fantastic to the mundane, the humor sometimes is less natural, a tad more bizarre. Here are the opening paragraphs from a chapter in *A Confederate General*, "The Tide Teeth of Lee Mellon":

It is important before I go any further in this military narrative to talk about the teeth of Lee Mellon. They need talking about. During these five years that I have known Lee Mellon, he has probably had 175 teeth in his mouth.

This is due to a truly gifted faculty for getting his teeth knocked out. It almost approaches genius. They say that John Stuart Mill could read Greek when he was three years old and had written a history of Rome at the age of six and a half.

This reversal doesn't work as humor quite as well as the previous example, because the neutral sentences are not part of the set-up, but are used to finish the joke. There's a deadpan humor to this strategy, of the bizarre masquerading as the everyday, but the implied connection between the historical fact of John Stuart Mill's genius and the asserted "genius" of Lee Mellon's losing his teeth either seems funny or it doesn't.

At his best, Brautigan doesn't allow that much leeway for the reader's responses.

Timing was an essential ingredient in Brautigan's finest writing, and he understood the virtues of the simple buildup. According to Virginia Alder, his first wife, and Brautigan's own account of his early apprenticeship as a writer, he worked for years at writing the simple sentences of his prose. In a notebook located in Brautigan's archive at UC Berkeley, an early draft of the chapter "Sea-Sea Rider" in *Trout Fishing* showed how he divided the prose into lines of verse, carefully trying to isolate each of the phrases by rhythm, by their cadence, revising for the simplest sound possible. Accompanying this draft is an aborted journal, written in 1960 and titled "August." In a rare moment of self-analysis, Brautigan wrote: "The idea of this journal is I want to make something other than a poem . . . One of the frustrations of my work is my own failure to establish adequate movement. . . . I want the reality in my work to move less obviously, and it [is] very difficult for me." What Brautigan means by movement is, I would guess, the switch from his metaphorical intelligence in and out of his mundane situations. In order to be less obvious, the transistion between the fantastic and quotidian had to be eased by giving both the same rhythms.

His poetry sometimes forced the connection between the mundane and his imaginative fancies by combining them in one sentence. The effect was artificial and clever, and so it lacked the careful, timed setups of his prose. What made his prose remarkable was his ability to sense those moments when his imagination could occupy the larger factual rhythms of his paragraphs. This might be what he meant by "adequate movement." When he strayed too far from the mundane and/ or factual setups, the cleverness had only itself to sustain, and his fiction suffered from the same defects as his poetry.

His fiction had its own peculiar vision and a sometimes satori-like sharpness. There's a humanity to Brautigan's discoveries which sets them apart from mere humorous writing. The opening paragraphs of the chapter, "Room 208, Hotel Trout Fishing In America," give a fine example of Brautigan's skills as a writer, how in a few words he could blend a prosaic vision of the world and at the same time infiltrate it with his own imagination and turn the mundane into something quicksilver, moving and alive.

Half a block from Broadway and Columbus is Hotel Trout Fishing in America, a cheap hotel. It is very old and run by some Chinese. They are young and ambitious Chinese and the lobby is filled with the smell of Lysol.

The Lysol sits like another guest on the stuffed furniture, reading a copy of the *Chronicle,* the Sports Section. It is the only furniture I have ever seen in my life that looks like baby food.

And the Lysol sits asleep next to an old Italian pensioner who listens to the heavy ticking of the clock and dreams of eternity's golden pasta, sweet basil and Jesus Christ.

THEMES

Trout Fishing In America was the first novel Brautigan wrote and, like most first novelists, he threw in the kitchen sink. He was in good company. F. Scott Fitzgerald made a mulligan stew of his first book. With a lot more class, Ernest Hemingway did the same in *The Sun Also Rises.* Fledgling novelists have felt a panic over deciding what goes in, and what to leave out, and often include everything currently on their minds. An author's prose style can strain, trying to include all his pressing concerns, but Brautigan did not try for a homogeneous narrative. I suspect that he did this because, given his over-active imagination, reading a book was not a homogeneous experience.

One way a writer approaches someone else's first novel is to skip-read through the opening lines of its chapters. With a remarkable and comic literalism, Brautigan starts his first chapter by talking about the cover, as if it were the first scene of the book. Of course, in an absolutely literal way, the cover is usually the first view we have of any novel.

The cover for *Trout Fishing* is a photograph taken late in the afternoon, a photograph of the Benjamin Franklin statue in San Francisco's Washington Square.

To talk about the cover in the first chapter is to insist on the present time of the reader. This insistence, and the casual aside "taken late in the afternoon" also tells us the author is concerned with the act of time's passing. The statue alerts us that he is equally concerned with a time past. This "dead" time can only be experienced by using emblems of the imagination like statues. For Brautigan, books are written statues which are always and forever set in the past, only coming alive at the moment of reading and then, the reading, the reader, and the book itself are as quickly part of the past.

This is a tight circle of associations. Brautigan was particularly attracted to circular motions and his prose moves in those ways. It could occur metaphorically, as in the opening paragraph from "The Last Mention of Trout Fishing in America Shorty":

Saturday was the first day of autumn and there was a festival being held at the church of Saint Francis. It was a hot day and the Ferris wheel was turning in the air like a thermometer bent in a circle and given the grace of music.

Or the circular motion could be a concept, as happens at the end of "Prologue to Grider Creek":

There's always a single feature, a double feature and an eternal feature playing at the Great theater in Mooresville, Indiana: the John Dillinger capital of America.

Rhetorical questions and figures of speech start some chapters. This, too, is typical of a first novel. First novels often record the trouble encountered while shedding the previous generation's flourishes. Brautigan proves no exception. *Trout Fishing* chapters begin with several such mannerisms. "As a child when did I first hear about trout fishing in America?" he asks no one in particular, striking a pose from a boy's novel. He quickly deflates this attitude with a story about his stepfather, "the old drunk," telling him about trout as if they were "a precious and intelligent metal."

A childhood hallucination, where some stairs become a trout stream, is followed by the introduction of the mythic god called Trout Fishing In America. The next chapter removes all possibilities of a Horatio Alger narrative with a mock Hemingway sentence. "Seventeen years later I sat down on a rock" neatly foreshortens the time between optimistic childhood and pessimistic adolescence. This is fooling around, but also a declaration of independence that *Trout Fishing* will not be a *bildungsroman* covering year X to year Y, but will hopscotch around as it pleases. Such a throwaway trope as the mock-elegiac "Gone now the old fart" opens another chapter, and what all this tells us is that the author is conscious about what he's writing while he writes it and he wants us to be so, too.

From chapter to chapter Brautigan's method of writing varies so much that it is difficult to find an exact description of this process. Some chapters are recipes, some catalogues, and some prose poems. Some chapters are popular forms of writing, such as the political diatribe or the letter from home. Brautigan's creation could be seen as similiar to what the folk art historians call piecing in quilting. In 1924 one Texas quilter, Mary Goodwin explained piecing this way.

> And then you're given just so much to work with in a life and you have to do the best you can with what you got. That's what piecing is. The material is passed on to you or is all you can afford to buy . . . that's just what's given you. Your fate. But the way you put them together is your business.

This could serve as a pretty fair country explanation for the process of accumulation that resulted in *Trout Fishing*. In a more literary vein, after beginning his writing career as a poet,

Brautigan habitually adapted poetic methods for his fiction, such as titling his short chapters as a poet names a lyric poem, to get the reader's attention and to set up expectations for the text. Unlike most chapter titles, they are designed to be provocative, to stop the reader for a second, rather than lead him on.

Brautigan was certainly cognizant of the stylistic collages of Pound, Olson and Williams but I doubt that he deliberately set out to write one. Probably the closest contemporary fictional models for Brautigan's mixture of poetry and prose were the poet Kenneth Patchen's anarchistic novel, *The Journal of Albion Moonlight* (which Brautigan mentions in *A Confederate General*) and Jack Spicer's mock narrative, *A Fake Novel about the Life of Arthur Rimbaud.*

Trout Fishing's returning, through-line characters are scarce. Two characters who do come back from time to time: Trout Fishing in America Shorty, a wino, and the mythic persona of Trout Fishing In America, an omniscient eternal god. These two provide the bottom and the top for Brautigan's social scale, bum and heroic god. The first person character rotates around in the middle. His age and situation change and his perceptions vary from poetic to mundane.

While the method of composition might be collage, *Trout Fishing's* narrative motion is that of a mobile, a circular collection of a motley and homegrown styles. Inside this mobile, Brautigan's themes turn and return, sometimes touching, sometimes not; connecting or diverging. The themes at times reach their resolution as style, and when attention is directed to the text itself, his style sometimes surfaces as a theme.

I thought to myself what a lovely nib trout fishing in America would make with a stroke of cool green trees along the river's shore, wild flowers and dark fins pressed against the paper.

Circularity is what makes Brautigan's fiction difficult to talk about. His themes are as restless and subversive as his style. As soon as one contains the other, there's a breakout or takeover.

One theme throughout Brautigan's work is that the imagination works as both a curse and a blessing. In his first two novels, *Trout Fishing in America* and *A Confederate General From Big Sur*, the imagination is presented as an uncontrollable force, from which people receive comfort, hope and despair. In all of his later work, this theme predominates, especially in his late 70s genre novels, *Sombrero Fallout* and *Dreaming of Babylon*. A cursed and runaway imagination's battle with reality also becomes the center for his last novel, published in 1984, *So The Wind Won't Blow It All Away*.

While the ability of the imagination to alter reality is celebrated, confusion breeds from it, too. In the second chapter of *Trout Fishing*, the child narrator imagines that trout are made of steel and that they represent the grand tradition of immigrant success like Andrew Carnegie. In a later chapter the child tries trout fishing using a slice of bread for bait and a safety pin for a hook. Carried away by his fervor to succeed, he hallucinates that "a flight of white wooden stairs" is a trout stream. In his disappointment the narrator says, "I ended up by being my own trout and eating the slice of bread myself." Dealing with reality becomes a matter of adjusting the imagination.

Brautigan showed how the imagination burgeons inside the mundane, widening what can be admitted as a possibility, until it sometimes parasitically grows to a point where the surrounding host structure (society, friendship, ethics, whatever) collapses, explodes or is consumed. His early fiction reflects his Northwest working-class roots. There Brautigan simply could not envision a society where imaginative effort was rewarded.

For Brautigan to imagine is to rebel and he is not alone in this view. In his discussion of the poet James Wright, Robert Hass writes:

> Over and over again in American writing, this theme or discovery, that the inner life has no place, that it makes outlaws of us. Whether it is Huck deciding to go to Hell

or the hell of West's *Miss Lonelyhearts.* . . . there is always
this sense of a radical division between the inner and
outer worlds and the hunger for a magic which will
heal it, a sanctification for election.

In the *Trout Fishing* chapter, "The Surgeon," the narrator talks to
a doctor who castigates society. The doctor claims its bureau-
cratic conformity is robbing him of his creative individuality
and peace of mind. The narrator says,

I talked to the surgeon for a little while longer and said
good-bye. We were leaving in the afternoon for Lake
Josephus, located at the edge of the Idaho Wilderness,
and he was leaving for America, often only a place in
the mind.

Imagination has another class function in Brautigan's writings,
too: it equals optimism. This is a distinctly American working-
class notion. *Trout Fishing* is filled with examples of this
equation. Andrew Carnegie's career remains a popular myth of
self-determination through imagination, one which Brautigan
was careful to place early in *Trout Fishing.* The anonymous man
in the first chapter who goes to the food handout expects to
find something more than a single spinach leaf in his sandwich.
Brautigan provides example after example of how imagination
and reality are seldom aligned, usually because exercising the
imagination admits to the hope that things will be different,
that the status quo won't do. While the longed-for top may be
money, fame or transcendence, the rise to it is only a thought
away.

Very few of Brautigan's characters ever win a lasting advantage using their imaginations. Usually they lose something, or
at best, merely cope with a situation. This bias accounts for the
many losers in Brautigan's writing. He was drawn to the failed
dreamers simply because they showed the most imagination.
To possess imagination is to be in ceaseless conflict with social
and economic worlds. When Brautigan imagines a genius at
work in the modern world, he can only come up with a slightly

bitter comedy about the commercial trivilization of talent: Leonardo da Vinci inventing a trout fishing lure, called The Last Supper, "far outstripping such shallow accomplishments as Hiroshima or Mahatma Ghandi."

Their imaginations spur Brautigan's characters into trying to succeed. But in some cases their social status provides only shopworn notions for their guides. In two of his best stories, he uses the most common transformation myths of America: first, everyone's got a story they can sell, and second, Hollywood will discover you. In "1/3, 1/3, 1/3," a logger hopes to turn into a novelist and make his life into a best seller. Brautigan carefully notes that the logger "looked like life had give him an endless stream of two-timing girlfriends, five-day drunks and cars with bad transmissions." In the story "Greyhound Tragedy," a woman dreams of a glamorous Hollywood life, but she can't ask the Greyhound clerk how much the bus ticket to Hollywood costs. The splendid vistas her imagination conjures only paralyze her.

More sophisticated concerns provide an impetus for another of Brautigan's themes. While his linguistic patterns were rooted in everyday American speech, he started writing as a poet and he grew up artistically in the milieu of the Black Mountain and Beat poetics. His fiction reflects a unique blend of these two influences. In the Beats' sociology, the artist is an alienated outsider with a surrealist vision. For the Black Mountain aesthetics, the way the information is *presented* often *is* the information (and Brautigan shares this stance), but he adapts this stylistic notion to fiction.

In his study of Brautigan, the French critic Chénetier describes this adaptation:

> Brautigan is a writer concerned with defying language's fixities and points of reference; indeed, I believe all his books are motivated by one central concern and activated by one central dialectic: they are driven by an obsessive interrogation of the fossilization and fixture of language, and by a counter-desire to free it from stultification and paralysis.

There's a problem with Brautigan's adoption of the Black Mountain aesthetic to his fiction. The moment when the verbal transformation becomes a dominant reality is volatile and fleeting. Poetry is usually the best way to enact it. If the fiction builds toward that moment, there is no interest in maintaining the usual dramatic situations, because the reader's attention is focused on the writer and his words, rather than his characters. This is why no fiction writers from the Black Mountain movement have achieved a popularity comparable to its poets. The aesthetic is not a dramatic one; it doesn't drive a narrative toward resolution. Any conclusion often remains open-ended, or returns the reader to the text.

This poetic bias creates a recurring structural pattern in Brautigan's novels and in turn becomes one of his themes: the transformation of being. Imagination dominates the characters' lives, imposing its own designs, irrespective of class or economic status. Being is perception, action and speech for Brautigan. Social status, possessions or money are dead and fixed; they are history, marble statues immutable except for the intervention of the living. For *A Confederate General's* down-and-out heroes, Lee Mellon and Jesse, the imagination's dominance over history is made early, when Big Sur is claimed as a member of the Confederate States of America. This grants them power over their own situation in a way that money or class can't. Indeed, at the end of the novel, $100,000 is thrown into the Pacific Ocean since it is useless to meet the demands of their present imagined reality.

Repeated throughout this novel is the theme: "Man is the dominant creature on this shitpile." That vulgarization of a scientific truth—humankind's glowing tribute to the powers of its own brain give rise to the comedy. This sentence starts out as an anthropological commonplace and ends in slang, miming a hidden working-class insistence that the highflown conceptions of science are sure to be brought down to earth by daily life.

Brautigan's first two novels develop similiar patterns of high and low. The term "Confederate General" acts in much the same way that the phrase "Trout Fishing in America" does. Lee

Mellon equals a Confederate General and represents an aristocratic rebel tradition. The character Trout Fishing in America idealizes pastoral America. Lee Mellon has a dual role; he is "a Confederate general in rags" and yet his daily life is roughly analogous to the character Trout Fishing in America Shorty, who represents "the cold turning of the earth, the bad wind that blows off sugar." The ideal and its representative reside in the same phrase and the same body and this creates conflict. The simultaneous burgeoning of both reality and imagination provides a maximum of friction between the ideal and its manifestations, and this dual flowering creates the drama between the characters and their situations. Any solutions are often outlandish. Lee Mellon finds the only thing that quiets the frogs in his pond is yelling "Campbell's Soup!" as he throws a rock into the water.

Coming from internal spontaneous processes, imagination often disrupts the surface of the story, too. Metaphors and similes introduce characters and cultures alien to the narrative.

> We neared our place late in the afternoon. Half a mile away there was a wooden bridge and a creek that flashed below. I was holding Elaine's hand. Like a bottle of beer in the haze the sun was plying its ancient Egyptian trade toward the end of the sky, the beginning of the Pacific ... Lee Mellon went and got a bottle of wine from the groceries and we walked out to the deck and toasted the sundown. The sun broke like a beer bottle on the water. We in a shallow sort of way reflected ourselves in the broken glass of the Egyptians. Each piece of Ra went away with a 60 horsepower Johnson outboard motor fastened to it.

Once all the characters are in Big Sur with Lee Mellon, the text itself enacts the disparity between imagination and reality. Split-screen dopplegangers disrupt the main story. Little histories appear at the end of chapters, acting as throwback codas for Lee's previous reincarnation. Brautigan imagines a Civil War history for Augustus Mellon, Lee's great-grandfather. He is not a Confederate general, but a foot soldier. This private faces some of the same problems as Lee in Big Sur: imagination interfering with reality.

> He came upon a Union captain lying headless among the flowers. With no eyes and no mouth, only flowers on top of the neck. The captain looked like a vase. But this did not distract Augustus Mellon to the point of not seeing the captain's boots. Though the captain's head was absent from this world, his boots were not, and they entertained the barefoot fantasies of Augustus Mellon's feet, and then replaced those fantasies with leather. Private Augustus Mellon left the captain even more deficient, even more unable to cope with reality.

Lee Mellon's grandiose notions of his grandfather's history were revealed as a momentary drunken aberration early on, and Lee shows no interest in the myth's continuance but his sidekick Jesse vows to maintain it. From then on, this notion's appearance is seldom determined by dramatic situation, or even Lee Mellon's mock-heroic actions, but becomes a metaphor for the entire book: life is a battle where imagination strains to resolve its contradictions. Sometimes, when the life is too hard, imagination supplants reality entirely. In this case, the little histories of Augustus Mellon provide an example of how little life has changed. Romance and grand gestures were absent then, too, despite the historical insistence that it was a grand and dashing time. Perhaps some balm comes with that notion.

In one of the endings for the novel, Jesse is exhausted with the outlandishness of their Big Sur life and he has a fantasy about a simple intuitive gesture that will give meaning to his life.

> A seagull flew over us. I reached up and ran my hand along his beautiful soft white feathers, feeling the arch and rhythm of his flight. He slipped off my fingers away into the sky.

This resolution of Jesse's conflict is effected by style, a trick of mind, rather than by catharsis. Fittingly enough, in *A Confederate General* the end also is rendered in a metaphor.

Then there are more and more endings: the sixth, the 53rd, the 131st, the 9,435th endings, endings going faster and faster, more and more endings, faster and faster until this book is having 186,000 endings per second.

Chénetier gives this interpretation for the situation in Brautigan's fiction:

The status of reality in Brautigan's novels and stories is always such that we cannot take them straightforwardly; rather than asserting the value of the real, these texts take their specific and unmistakable quality from a persistent speculation on the very nature of the real, as well as of textual activity itself.

Brautigan's interrogation of style contains its virtues and defects, since little dramatic satisfaction issues from such resolutions in his fiction. But, in Brautigan's view, reality is largely shifting and uncertain and this is compounded by the constant play of the imagination. When imagination does stop, instantly things turn to marble, are dead, ossified. Brautigan celebrates that there is no common society, no history, which cannot be altered, destroyed, ignored or rendered impotent by the imagination. Chénetier calls this trait of Brautigan's, "... a willful violation of reality." Whenever history is retold, the imagination is free to fiddle with it, as in the first chapter of *A Confederate General*:

It was during the second day of the Battle of the Wilderness. A.P. Hill's brave but exhausted Confederate Troops had been hit at daybreak by Union General Hancock's II Corps of 30,000 men. A.P. Hill's troops were shattered by the attack and fell back in defeat and confusion along the Orange Plank Road.

Twenty-eight-year-old Colonel William Poague, the South's fine artillery man, waited with sixteen guns in one of the few clearings in the Wilderness, Widow Tapp's farm. Colonel Poague had his guns loaded with antipersonnel ammunition and opened fire as soon as A.P. Hill's men had barely fled the Orange Plank Road.

The Union assault funneled itself right into a vision of sculptured artillery fire, and the Union troops suddenly found pieces of flying marble breaking their center and breaking their edges. At the instant of contact, history transformed their bodies into statues. They didn't like it, and the assault began to back up along the Orange Plank Road. What a nice name for a road.

The present intrudes in Brautigan's work, and the present is defined as the moment of writing itself, the "real" present for the writer. This insistence can be seen as egocentric, which it certainly is, but it also can be seen as existentially truthful. The ultimate reality of any text, for Brautigan, is the moment it is written.

Brautigan's own kind of Heisenbergian Uncertainty Principle functions in his work. Style measures content, and since that physical process of writing alters the product, Brautigan asks the question, Well, why not record that, too? While Brautigan sees that his imagination can make history come alive, he simultaneously mourns that imagination will also inevitably warp events in the telling. This constant circle between the author's present time and his simultaneous fossilization in style creates a poignant push and pull across the surface of his fiction. Indeed, in *Trout Fishing*, he imagines the central metaphor of the book becoming a pen to magically write the entire book, with its style being nature itself on the pages.

I thought to myself what a lovely nib trout fishing in America would make with a stroke of cool green trees along the river's shore, wild flowers and dark fins pressed against the paper.

This stylistic push-pull flows into another of Brautigan's themes, the problem of rendering things exactly, even down to keeping the original energy of the events intact. From *Trout Fishing's* narrator's account of his youthful introduction to the notion of a historical reality for trout:

> As a child when did I first hear about trout fishing in America? From whom? I guess it was a stepfather of mine.
> Summer of 1942.
> The old drunk told me about trout fishing. When he could talk, he had a way of describing trout as if they were precious and intelligent metal.
> Silver is not a good adjective to describe what I felt when he told me about trout fishing.
> I'd like to get it right.

The wish to assume control over history, and his sadness over the attempts to get things right, recalls a Zen phrase for this process, *jushaku shoshaku.* This can be translated, "wave after wave of error." In this phrase, error can also be understood as illusion. This sense of the world's endless capacity for misleading us is what so closely ties Brautigan's work with Buddhism—one reason why his fiction became so popular in Japan. Since in Buddhist terms all is illusion, time becomes ahistorical. There is a now, and that is all. In discussing Yasunari Kawabata's work in *Beauty and Sadness,* Roger Scruton makes some useful distinctions about what this ahistorical point of view means for fiction:

> ...his characters take what life they have from situations where historical continuity can play no significant role. Thus he showed little interest in marriage, in the relation of parent to child, in the struggle of men for influence, power and understanding. All those activities and institutions which entail, in their dramatic realization, a necessary consciousness of history, remain untreated in his novels, and if

Kawabata occasionally refers to them it is with a distant, haiku-like allusiveness.

This could stand as a description of Brautigan's fiction. The usual sources for fiction's dramatic structure, the referential activities and institutions of historical people, are never really used in Brautigan's novels to bind the narratives together. If Brautigan's novels are ahistorical, as are Kawabata's works, with nothing more central than the moment-to-moment consciousness of the characters, the unifying element becomes style, or how one imaginatively perceives and/or records each moment. Unlike Kawabata's fiction, though, in Brautigan's work there is little serenity to this process. Chénetier gets to the center of the conflict.

On one hand he feels a compulsive fascination for the written—or rather for that being written, for writing as act—and a hope that anything written might just succeed in perpetuating the moment; on the other hand, he feels a fascinated repulsion, because at the same moment writing is killing. The result is a very active polarity which is far more than the classic "life and death" preoccupation of so much writing. Here it is a tension between writing as life and the written object as cemetery, corpse or grave.

The curse and blessing of the imagination is that the mind wants to create an autonomous object, yet it can't prevent itself from imagining that object's eventual disintegration and it can't fail to understand that by giving birth to something, that something's death is assured. Brautigan's tragedy, which he enacted in book after book and eventually in his own life, was that he defined everything, including himself, in terms of an ahistorical imagination. Brautigan wanted to round up life in one mercurial, moving, magic vision, but he recognized that he could produce only "paper phantoms," his term for books.

Once, while cleaning out the trout before I went home

in the almost night, I had a vision of going over to the poor graveyard and gathering up grass and fruit jars and tin cans and markers and wilted flowers and bugs and weeds and clods and going home and putting a hook in the vise and tying a fly with all that stuff and then going outside and casting it up into the sky, watching it float over clouds and then into the evening star.